Swarthmore Lecture 1981

TRUE JUSTICE

Quaker peace makers and peace making

by Adam Curle

True justice is the harvest reaped by peace makers from seeds sown in a spirit of peace—*James, 3:18 (NEB)*

The joining of hands to dissolve barriers of age, race or sex, hatred, fear or ignorance is the foundation of real peace, the source of true justice

D1152436

QHS

QUAKER HOME SERVICE · LONDON

First published May 1981

ISBN 0 85245 156 3

Cover design by John Blamires
Photograph by Christina Goldfine

Printed in Great Britain in 11/12 Photon Times
by Headley Brothers Ltd., The Invicta Press,
Ashford, Kent and London

PREFACE

The Swarthmore Lectureship was established
by the Woodbrooke Extension Committee at a
meeting held December 9th, 1907: the minute
of the Committee providing for 'an annual
lecture on some subject relating to the message
and work of the Society of Friends'. The name
Swarthmore was chosen in memory of the
home of Margaret Fox, which was always open
to the earnest seeker after Truth, and from
which loving words of sympathy and
substantial material help were sent to fellow
workers.

The lectureship has a twofold purpose: first, to
interpret further to the members of the Society
of Friends their message and mission; and,
secondly, to bring before the public the spirit,
the aims and fundamental principles of Friends.
The lecturer alone is responsible for any
opinions expressed.

The lectureship provides both for the publication
of a book and for the delivery of a lecture, the
latter usually at the time of assembly of London
Yearly Meeting of the Society of Friends. A lecture
related to the present book was delivered at
Friends House, Euston Road, London, on
the evening of May 22nd, 1981.

*To my daughter Christina Goldfine,
whose skills provided the
photographs and whose family form
the subject of the front cover, in
gratitude for love and friendship*

ACKNOWLEDGEMENTS

I am immeasurably privileged to have had the experience of people and affairs on which this lecture is based. I have been given much by the Friends with whom I have had the honour to work; by the women and men I have met in circumstances of oppression and violence; by colleagues from whom I learned some skills of social and psychological analysis; by teachers who passed on their understanding of the nature of things; by my incomparable wife, children, grandchildren and friends, whose love gently pierced the carapace of self and illusion.

In all this I have been greatly blessed by God and feel there is nothing more I would wish to say about my life.

Among Friends who have been particularly involved, directly or indirectly, with the work reported here, I must express my love and gratitude to Ruth and Nicholas Gillett, Walter Martin, Trish Swift, Margery and Roger Wilson, and Mike Yarrow; I have already mentioned my wife, Anne, who has been concerned with every aspect of the work and has accompanied me on many of the journeys. I also want to thank warmly Cecil Evans, Roger Iredale, Nancy

McCrae, Paul and Ann Nash, James O'Connell, and Andrew Tatham who kindly read the manuscript (as also did Anne, Roger and Mike, to whom I have already referred). I am also most grateful to George Gorman, to whom I am indebted in many ways, Clifford Barnard, and members of the Swarthmore Lecture Committee who read and made valuable comments on the draft.

Adam Curle

CONTENTS

INTRODUCTION

When people learn that I have been involved in peace studies, they react in several different ways. Some are scathingly amused, some simply scornful, some mystified, some embarrassingly deferential. The ones I find it hardest to answer are those who assume that I have, or think I have, some formula for making peace; and they usually also assume that I am only concerned with international, or perhaps also industrial, peace.

I try to explain that I am as much concerned with the human condition in general as with specific conflicts, which often represents only the tip of a pyramid of violence and anguish. I say that I am concerned with all the pain and confusion that impede our unfolding and fulfilment. Often, of course, circumstances force us to focus on extreme examples of unpeacefulness. However, if we were to limit our attention to these, we would be neglecting the soil out of which they grow and would continue to grow until the soil were purified. In this sense the social worker, the teacher, the wise legislator, or the good neighbour is just as much a peace maker as the woman or man unravelling some lethal international imbroglio.

My questioners are seldom satisfied with this. They expect me to come up with a recipe for peace, if only for the gratification of demolishing it. My problem, however, is that real, root issues are as complex and profound as life itself. It may be easy enough (although certainly not always) to stop two individuals fighting or two nations quarrelling. But does that mean peace has been achieved? We have to ask searching questions about the meaning of peace, the realities of human nature, the essence of justice, the right ordering of society, the relationship of God and our-

1

selves (that is, if we believe in God; if we don't, the other questions are still relevant). To say anything worth saying about peace we have to try to say something about life. This is not easy in a lecture, still less in a casual conversation.

In this essay I have tried to speak to these issues, and indeed to many others. I begin with a concept of human nature based on the belief that there is within each one of us a divine element. I go on to develop ideas on peace making that seem to me to follow from this. Finally I try to suggest how our action as peace makers is influenced by a combination of our understanding of our natures and our analysis of the situation. (I use the rather pretentious term peace maker perhaps too freely. But I mean by it anyone, and that means all of us some of the time, who is trying to reduce disharmony and restore love. I maintain that peace making is a natural and important human function.)

This brief outline will suggest that I shall try to weave together some aspects of two great themes of Quaker faith and witness; the belief in that of God in every one and the Peace Testimony that seems to flow so inescapably from it. I pray I have not been presumptuous.

I should also mention what I do not discuss, which many may feel to be a serious omission. However, I am constrained by the limitations of my experience which, so far as practical peace making is concerned, is mainly as a mediator attempting to find ways of bringing people together. To a number of Friends, the main thrust of peace work relates to the promotion of disarmament and human rights, opposition to the arms trade and to militarism at home and abroad, and the establishment of a more equitable society. I share their belief in the crucial urgency of these matters, but have relatively little experience of them—certainly not enough on which to base a Swarthmore Lecture.

I concentrate, necessarily, on a narrower field. I hope, however, that the general principles considered may be appropriate to most types of peace work. In particular, the section on the Stages of Quiescence and of Revolution may be relevant to issues of changing attitudes and social structures that underlie concerns for peace, in whatever way they are manifested.

I was invited to write this lecture and indeed had completed a rough draft, before the dramatic and dangerous deterioration of relationships between the super powers that became apparent early in 1980. I debated whether I should rewrite the lecture in the light of the crisis into which we had slid, but decided not to. The current instability, I argued, did not indicate a radical change in the global situation. The rivalries, the nationalistic greed, the paranoia, the atrocious arsenals had been there all along, but we had been sedated into forgetfulness. Moreover, the relative quiescence of Europe and North America helped us to ignore the turmoil and bloodshed in so many parts of the Third World during recent decades—we are at peace, we foolishly thought. We are not now faced, it seems to me, with an essentially new situation, but with a rearrangement and intensification of what was there before. I hope that the general themes of this essay are as appropriate to the current situation as to the ones that both preceded and will succeed it.

Rather than distract the reader with references to all the many quotations, which are intended to evoke a mood or emphasise a meaning rather than as a scholarly exercise, I have included a bibliography. This lists most of the books that have had the greatest influence on my thinking about the main themes of this book, as well as almost all of those from which I have quoted. I have grouped them in three categories: spiritual writings; writings on the controversy about human nature, both for and against the view I espouse; works on non-violence, social change and awakening awareness.

Most of the few footnotes refer the reader to an item in the bibliography.

I

THE NATURE OF HUMAN NATURE

What is our nature? Are we, as Robert Ardrey* and some of the ethologists would have us believe, killer apes (oddly enough, for apes are gentle creatures) dominated by violent and aggressive instinctual drives? Or, as some behaviourists would maintain, beings who can be conditioned to anything and so are devoid of any natural tendencies for good (or, presumably, ill). Or, as a social philosopher like Hobbes believed, destined to a life that was 'nasty, poor, solitary, brutish and short'? Or, as some theologians would have us think, so enmired in original sin that 'there is no health in us'?

Or are we made in the image and likeness of God, bearing the Seed, the Divine Principle, illuminated by the Light of Christ within. Virtually the sole dogma, if this word is not too emphatic, of Friends concerns 'that of God in every one' and this has, of course, dominated our witness. However, I am happy to learn that the indwelling divinity seems to be a part of all the great religions. The Gospels, the Pauline epistles and the writings of the Christian mystics are permeated with this belief. 'The Kingdom of God is within you', said Jesus; 'Ye are the temple of God', wrote St Paul; 'The centre of the soul is God' wrote St John of the Cross; 'to gauge the soul we must gauge it with God, for the Ground of the Soul and the Ground of God

---

* The bibliography includes a short section listing some of the works dealing with the scientific (as opposed to theological or philosophical) aspect of the controversy over the nature of human nature. Montague and Maslow take a point of view approximately opposite to that of Ardrey, Lorenz and Morris. Fromm and Storr are more or less in the middle.

are the same'—this from Meister Eckhart; 'my me is God', said St Catherine of Genoa, 'nor do I recognise any other Me except my God himself'. Surely the living and working of the Holy Spirit in each of us ('it is no longer I who live, but Christ lives in me' said St Paul) is the foundation of Christianity. And I am fascinated to learn that Jelal ud-din Rumi said 'Jesus is within you: seek his aid'.

Nor do we have to seek far to find equivalent beliefs in other religions. 'He who knows himself knows God' said Mohammad and this is echoed by many of the Sufis. Ana al-Haqq (I am the truth or the real—a popular Sufi synonym for God) proclaimed Al-Hallaj, though entirely without the blasphemous intent for which the orthodox barbarously slew him. He also wrote: 'I am He whom I love, and he whom I love is I; we are two spirits in one body. If you see me, you see him. And if you see Him, you see us both'. Compare Jan van Ruysbroeck: 'God in the depth of us receives God who comes to us; it is God contemplating God'. The gentle Kabir, who linked the mystical faiths of Hinduism and Islam wrote: 'Until you have found God in your own soul, the whole world will seem meaningless to you'.

In Hinduism, the concept of Atman represents both the source of all being, Brahman, the Absolute, and its individualised expression. The Brihad-arankya Upanishad speaks of it thus: 'he is yourself, the Inner Controller' and the Vedic seers proclaimed 'Aham Brahmasi—I am Brahman'. Tat Tvam Asi is the refrain of the Chandogya Upanishad: 'Thou art that'—thou art, in Quaker terms, the Inner Light; it is your essence.

Moreover, so far as I can grasp the subtleties of the Tao, it is the message of Chuang Tzu. 'He who is the servant of God knows that the son of heaven and himself are equally the children of God'. And the Buddhists recognise in all the existence of the Buddha nature.

Here, then, is a different understanding of our nature, a nature grounded in God and hence in a mystery that cannot be directly described, but only partially conveyed through allegory or great art, very often in allegories of human love; our most intense experience of joy would seem to foreshadow what has been known transcendentally to the mystics. Moreover, our attempts to describe mystical experiences are filtered through different cultures and traditions. Yet the fundamental areas of unity of, for example, Suso, William Law, the author of *The Cloud of Unknowing*, Bayazid of Bistam, Farid ud-din Attar, Shankara and the teachings of the *Bhagavad Gita* shine through the great diversity of idiom.

But there is a third way of considering our nature. We are the psalmist's Manichean mixture of good and evil, truth and false-hood: 'Ye are gods; and all of you are children of the most high, but ye shall die like men'. Or Pascal: 'What a chimera is man. What a novelty. What a monster, what a chaos, what a contra-diction, what a prodigy. Judge of all things, imbecile, worm of the earth; depository of truth, sink of uncertainty and error; the pride and refuse of the universe'. It would be a rash man who tried to hack through this tangled and thorny psychological, biological, philosophical and theological thicket. The wisest polymath could hardly escape laceration. It seems to me, however, that the ample evidence can be argued in many different ways. Once we have studied it as honestly as we can, avoiding dubious facts and faulty logic, we are bound to reach conclusions based on experience and values—and these, of course, we must also subject to rigorous examination.

We must admit, firstly, that there is all too much evidence to suggest that human nature is flawed by violence and aggression, and that these are fuelled by such emotions as greed, vanity, pride, envy and fear. (It is interesting, incidentally, that in American usage, aggressive means 'vigorously energetic' and is applied as a compliment. I believe it is only when this expression of striving for self-realisation is frustrated, that it sours into the English sense of violent and destructive.) But does the fact that we so often behave badly mean that we have built-in biological characteristics of violence and destructiveness? History tells us a story which is in large part, but by no means exclusively, discouraging, but some of the archaeological and palaeontological evidence for our innate violence is flimsy. The practice of cannibalism, especially as suggested by archaeological findings, has, for example, been quoted as proof of our violence towards each other. But ample anthropological data show that in both ancient and in more or less contemporary society, the practice has been predominantly ritualistic, an act of piety towards one's own people or of revenge against enemies. The apparent universality of war is also often used to demonstrate the universality of human violence. In the simplest societies, however, it often does not (or did not) exist at all. In fact what might be thought of as the most 'natural' human beings did not fight each other collectively. Slightly more complex societies have had a ritualised form of warfare more like a sporting event than the butchery we know as war. In some tribes the arrows, unlike those used for hunting, are feathered so that they will not fly straight. In others, the opponents hurl spears at each other, but are careful to position themselves just out of range. In yet others, the fight is called off as soon as anyone is hurt. What we would recognise as war seems only to have begun on a large scale when the early wandering food gatherers became settled agriculturalists. Then communities began to compete for land, water supplies and other resources. In fact, a study of 652 pre-literate societies* shows that only one-third engaged in anything like warfare. A third type of argument, based on applying to human beings principles derived

---

* T. Broch and J. Galtung, 'Belligerence among Primitives' in *Journal of Peace Research*, vol. III, no. 1, pp. 35-45, 1966.

from observation of animal behaviour must be considered questionable. There is no adequate evidence that one can extrapolate from animal to human behaviour. It is interesting, incidentally, that anthropologists, who study human society, tend to take a more optimistic view of our nature than do those ethologists who generally concentrate on animals. Since animals, on the whole, are much less violent than we are, this is rather strange!

I would add one further argument against those who would see us as incurably violent. If there are any genuine exceptions they must argue against the universality of the characteristic— here the exception emphatically does not prove the rule. I say 'genuine' advisedly, because an exception may be apparent rather than real. For example, a society, may be seemingly non-violent because there are very strong sanctions against the expression of hostility. Or an individual may seem to be lacking in aggression because s/he is frightened of her/his inner violence, as a good Freudian might argue. But a people like the Tasaday,* recently discovered in the Philippines, appear to have had no idea that human beings could ever wish to hurt each other. And have we not all known people whose lovingness and gentleness were unthinkable as a substitute for suppressed violence?

However, although I do not believe that the extreme ethological views can be maintained, there is certainly a case to consider. I don't believe that this has as much to do with the 'animal' aspect of our nature, as with its machine-like quality. In a sense our intelligence resembles that of a computer. A vast amount of information is constantly fed into the data bank of our memory at many levels of consciousness. When we need to act, and the action may be as simple as scratching, or as

---

* Described in *The Gentle Tasaday* by John Nance. London: Gollancz, 1975.

complex as driving a car or writing a book, the necessary information is retrieved instantaneously and we act on it. But false or destructive information (prejudices, misconceptions, errors of fact, artificial needs, prides, resentments, the exaggerated memories of old pains, every sort of bigoted and harmful ism) are fed into the bank as well as what is useful and time-saving— consider how difficult life would be if we had to re-learn to use a knife and fork every time we ate! The false or distorted information is retrieved by the appropriate stimulus in just the same way as that which is correct. Thus very often a quite unsuitable response is made automatically to a situation requiring judgement and careful thought. Sometimes we realise almost immediately, and regret, the automatic impulse that made us act stupidly or speak harshly. Sometimes we have become so machine-like, so unaware, that we never fully realise the harm we have done. In these cases the machine function, which exists to help us act more effectively, has taken over the human being. When this happens, as it does to all of us some of the time at least, it is not hard to believe that there is something inherently bad in human nature.

This has important implications for some later arguments that I will mention only briefly at this point. The more we are dominated by the machine functions, with the constant chatter of their flow of associations, the less are we in touch with the deeper part of the self, the ground of the soul. This, of course, is why the silence of the meeting for worship is so crucial to our well being; in quietness we come close to our real nature, and hence to God. ('Be still and know that I am God', said the psalmist; 'Quietness is the master of the deed' teaches the Tao Te Ching.) In noise we become lost, machines without a driver.

Of course, we are never wholly automatic, completely unaware; just as we are perhaps never fully awake to our natures. Hence Pascal's anguished dualism.

How, then, about the mystical approach? I cannot *prove* its truth any more than I can *prove* the existence of God, the immortality of the soul, or the power of love. But then I can't either prove that the pen with which I am writing or the chair in which I am sitting are what they appear to be. Indeed, I am told they are arrangements of evanescent sub-atomic particles, fields of energy that our sense organs and brains (similarly formed) invest with a particular sort of meaning. All I can say is that this meaning suits my purpose very well and that the mystical approach strikes a deep chord within me. I feel it to be right and the conviction has grown steadily over the years. No one, moreover, has been able to show me any good reason for not believing in the reality of the Inner Light (and as an academic I am perhaps too inclined, at least my wife tells me so, to heed reason rather than faith).

I believe that if we fully know, feel, realise, understand and are immersed in the reality of the God who forms part of us, and so of whom we form a tiny fragment, everything will change. We shall become the human beings we were created to be (and perhaps in the becoming lies the purpose of our creation). We shall awake. This is an important word. When Jesus chided the disciples because they slept in the Garden of Gethsemane, 'could you not watch and pray with me?', he perhaps reproached them less for failure to keep physically awake than to remain aware, recollected. And on another occasion he admonished: 'I say unto you all, watch'. It is interesting that the word Buddha comes from the root BUDH which implies being watchful, aware; and the Dhammapada tells us 'watchfulness is the path of immortality; unwatchfulness is the path of death. Those who are watchful never die; those who do not watch are already as dead'. 'There is no death but negligence in recollection', said Shankara '... through this a man is distracted from awareness of his divine nature'. And more or less in our own day Thoreau wrote: 'To be awake is to be alive. I have never yet met a man who was quite awake'. If we can remain awake we shall effectively use the superb machine that is our body without being dominated by its automatic functions; we shall use them. If we are aware, we shall be alive every moment.

In the next chapter I shall explore the implications, for ourselves and others, of believing, in the sense of knowing experientially and with certainty, in the divine basis of our nature. I respect those who say of Christian dogma, *Credo quia impossibile*. But this is not enough. 'I believe because I know' is more powerful. There is, I believe, spiritually irrefutable knowledge of that of God within us; and for those who know, this tremendous fact must be the most important thing in the world. What else could match its towering significance? It must form the foundation of our attitude towards ourselves and towards those others to whom we are joined, being all children of God. Nor do I mean this as a pious figure of speech. I mean that we share the same source and so, in a very real sense, are one, although we are also unique and individual expressions of the infinite attributes of God. We represent a miracle of unity in diversity. I shall try to explain that if we really sense that of God in every one of us, the conventions of human relations, individual and social, must be radically altered. Although much that is good and co-operative has become institutionalised, so has much that is completely incompatible with our real relationship one to another. Recognition of our shared brotherhood and sisterhood must lead to the disappearance of injustices of caste and class, of snobbery and elitism, of 'enlightened self-interest', let alone exploitation, oppression and everything that comes from those false beliefs by which we exalt or justify ourselves and deride or degrade others.

So acknowledgement of our true selves is revolutionary. It must lead to great changes. It must also lead to peace, since the antithesis to peace is created by the greed, envy, fear and hatred that stem from a false understanding.

Thus the search for peace and the recognition of reality are identical. To become our proper selves and to serve as peace makers are essential human tasks, common to us all. Each one of us can exercise them in our different spheres. In the same sense we all exercise psychological judgements about the human situations we are involved with; we all make administrative decisions about issues in family, work, or neighbourhood; we all make decisions about what is right or wrong, just or unjust. So do psychologists and psychiatrists, administrative and management experts, politicians, and lawyers and judges. In doing this they use, or should do, a body of systematic information, but their decisions may be less wise than those of the lay person. Thus my wife is a much better practical psychologist than I am although I know more about the theory and have even held a chair in the subject. Nevertheless, there should be no inconsistency between the knowledge of the specialist and that of the layman or woman; the approach of the one should complement that of the other. I would like to emphasise this. We rely too much on 'experts' and I should be very sad if something as important and universal as peace making became their prerogative.

In the third chapter there will be a somewhat systematic and theoretical discussion of concepts related to peace and peace making. This inevitably reflects my understanding of our nature. Because of my views there are some approaches to peace I could never countenance and in fact believe to be profoundly unpeaceful: 'peace' achieved by pounding the opposition into submission; 'peace' maintained by crushing protest against injustice; 'peace' for the rulers at the expense of the misery of the ruled. More positively, I define peace as a situation that helps to free us from whatever impedes our unfolding, as circumstances in which the Inner Light joins the outer and in which the Seed germinates. Naturally I try to write as objectively as possible about peace problems and to clarify terms and concepts that are controversial or ambiguous. In general I try to describe the issues that the would-be peace maker must be prepared to tackle.

The fourth and fifth chapters constitute a sort of manual for peace makers who base their actions on a particular set of spiritual values and beliefs. I attempt to describe how peace makers who believe that our nature is fundamentally perfect may act. I have already, in Chapter Two, said what this might imply for their attitudes; now it is a question of how their behaviour may be influenced. Note that I am talking of those who believe, as Friends may, together with other Christians, not to speak of Buddhists, Hindus and others, that our nature already *is* perfect. Those who hold that it is imperfect, but is perfectible through prayer, fasting, good works, or Divine Grace, may behave differently. Those who hold that we are at best *tabula rasa* and at worst intrinsically evil may have few scruples about how to obtain peace on their own terms; as Tacitus said, they will make a desert and call it peace.

At this point I should like to clarify what may seem a controversial statement: that our nature is perfect. If we believe, as Friends do, with many others (some of them are quoted in this chapter) that the ground of the soul is God, this divine ground must be the fundamental reality of our being, the true self beside which all else is triviality, error, or illusion. It is God's creation: how could it be flawed? There is, of course, a sad disparity between what we *are*, as creatures made in God's image, and what we *do*. Theologians of all ages and many religions have grappled with this contradiction and I have neither the ability nor the inclination to enter into the debate. The essence of my faith is rooted in experience and so, like much Quaker belief, can

14

be neither proved nor disproved by doctrinal argument. I try, however (pages 9 and 10 and in the section that now follows), to describe part of the mechanism of our bad behaviour. I cannot presume to say anything about the *reason* for it, any more than I can explain how a God of love created a world in which there is evil and suffering.

Roots of Violence

To conclude this discussion of human nature, I should try to identify some of the roots of violence. These must be eradicated if peace is more widely to prevail. As I have already said, much of our behaviour is dominated by automatic responses to stimuli that activate our 'computer'. Not only are such responses completely inadequate ways of behaving towards other human beings, but the more automatic and unconscious the more likely to be based on old hurts or confusions and so to be irrational or reactively violent. In such automatic responses we express what we have learned, but not learned usefully in the way that enables us to swim, ride a bicycle, or speak a foreign language after years without practice. What we learn as the result of distress or ignorance are the complexes of fixed ideas about people and society often referred to as isms. These memory traces of fear, rejection, humiliation, loneliness and other painful feelings not only warp our human relations, but evoke actions that range from being inappropriate or self-damaging to being in varying degrees destructive—which of course further distorts our relations.

The greed and selfishness that are so sadly prevalent and taint so much of human existence develop, at least in part, from the need to compensate for what is dimly felt to be wrong with us. This is a spiritual want, but we seldom see it like this—if we did, everything would be different. As it is, the more uneasy we feel, the more, in our anxiety, do we become automatic and so further estranged from our true nature. The more machine-like our behaviour, the more are we torn by largely unconscious conflicts, the more we experience a feeling of worthlessness, a flawed identity—and the more desperate our efforts to make up for these lacks.

Our compensatory quest for material success or advantage, on however modest a scale, is an attempt to establish a new identity, one based on material rather than spiritual values. As such it is clearly most vulnerable—we can fall ill, or lose our money overnight. However, the more it is threatened, the more we struggle to defend it, and the greater our hostility towards those who appear to menace it.

A closely intertwined root of violence, is ignorance or virtual ignorance of our nature. If we don't know fully that the ground of our nature is divine, there is little to guide us except that our nature, working secretly, may indicate the path. To the extent that we are ignorant, we are led to a life of illusion dominated by the appearances of the material world. Once we lose the sense of inhabiting a universe in which literally everything emanates from God ('God', said Isaac Penington, is 'the inward substance of all that appears'), we begin to separate the material from the divine, making the material important in its own right. It is then that we become accustomed to the idea of gaining or maintaining material things, such as territory, or wealth, or privilege, by violence.

This, in fact, is the basis of a highly materialistic philosophy (I don't call it materialism, since this term has a specific meaning in philosophical usage). It is a way of thinking that, allowing for differences in culture, I have met in so many societies that it seems almost ubiquitous. Moreover, we all share in it to some extent, although Quakers collectively perhaps less than most; certainly members of some Christian denominations might consider it perfectly legitimate.

A number of things follow from belief in the fundamental imperfections of human nature, and in the reality and importance of the material world that provides a substitute means of measuring our value.

First, it justifies violence: the ends are more important than those who may stand in the way of achieving them.

Then it accords respect to hierarchy and all the paraphernalia of rank as indicators of success. By the same token, it confirms our own status by according inferior positions to, for example, women, people of other races, colours or classes or of apparently lower intelligence, to the poor, etc. This also exalts convention, since it is convention that maintains these standards of judgement—I do not imply that the philosophy is necessarily conservative in any ordinary sense (although it may be), but that the particular orthodoxies of the group, even if *avant garde* or revolutionary, assume great significance.

In the broadest sense, things mean more than people and the value of people is further diminished if they do not behave rightly towards things, are lacking in patriotism, for example, or whatever is the appropriate *esprit de corps*.

A particularly dangerous and unsavoury aspect of this philosophy is its sanctification of 'interests', personal or national, in the defence of which any enormity, including nuclear war, is acceptable.

It is a strange paradox that this type of materialist outlook both separates us from each other, in the sense of emphasising our own interests and the selfish means by which they may be enhanced; and ties us to the group, but as an entity that helps us to define our precarious identities rather than as a collection of individuals with whom we have personal ties.

In the next chapter, we shall consider a very different philosophy, one with which we are also all acquainted and, I imagine, more closely. Unlike what I have just been describing, it is a peaceful philosophy based on awareness and understanding rather than automatism and ignorance.

There is also a collective level of violence in which individuals may take part whether or not they have any strong personal tendencies towards violence. This is because, over long periods of time the psychological roots of violence, individual greed, fear, rapacity, selfishness, coupled with dependence on and belief in the power and worth of the material, have become institutionalised. Armies have been created to defend the state (itself a highly materialistic concept) or extend its boundaries; traditions of national, racial, or religious superiority and prejudice have grown up; empires have been created and dominate their subject peoples; huge and exploitative economic structures have evolved. These vast edifices function irrespective, to a large extent, of the individuals who comprise them (who has not known a kindly and generous capitalist or a peaceable soldier?), but it is understandably hard for those individuals and indeed everyone, including all of us, not to be influenced by the institutions in whose shadow they live and work.

Such are the roots of violence in ourselves and our society. I firmly deny that they are intrinsic to our nature, but they are deep and all pervasive. They are comparable to the Hindu concept of maya, illusion; something omnipresent although ultimately not real, something we must pass beyond. All peace makers must, of course, be concerned about these issues and their effects and I have sometimes wondered whether I should not be devoting the whole of this lecture (and indeed of my life) to the eradication of this fundamental source of violence, advocating prayer or psychotherapy at the individual level, and on the larger scale, social and political action aimed at dismantling or changing institutions that promote or support violence.

I refrained for three reasons. First, I could not do it properly.

I think I have a reasonable idea of what is wrong, but how to change it and with what to replace it, I cannot so easily tell. Beyond recommending, for example, cooperative rather than competitive practices, the elimination of gross inequalities, and universal disarmament, I have little original or helpful to suggest. I could too easily get caught up in vaguely abstract panaceas, forgetting the few practical things I might be able to say.

Second, I trust that all Friends and all people of insight and goodwill are in any case working for peace in their own ways, hoping to dry up the springs of violence in themselves and their communities. There is so much to be done at all levels and of every sort, and everyone's potentiality is different. Any attempt to define and codify roles would merely constitute a limitation.

Third, although I have confined my comments to peace making in more specifically unpeaceful situations rather than to the ground from which they grow, much of what I have to say does relate to the ground. The emphasis on awareness, on recognition of 'that of God' within, on listening, on social change, on the elimination of social injustices and structural violence, must affect more basic matters than a particular quarrel.

II

THAT OF GOD

In order to apprehend the divine in others, we must recognise it in ourselves. But it is somehow easier, at least for me, to accept that others are the daughters and sons of God than that I am. When others are unkind, foolish or downright bad we can make excuses for them—they were worried, ill-informed, had an unhappy childhood, were under strain, etc. Where we ourselves are concerned, however, we are all too aware of the trivial thoughts, the dubious motives, the laziness, vanity, greed and so on. How can we believe in that of God in ourselves? What shred of evidence have we?

Well, to start with, we have other people. We may be aware of their flaws, but the more profoundly we know them, the more we see miraculous qualities. When they might have been expected to curse, they speak with charity; when they might have been expected to give up, they are steadfast; when they might have been expected to hate, they love. Against every deterministic pressure, they demonstrate their freedom. I see in these people a wisdom that is deep, penetrating and compassionate. I see a strength manifested in vivid aliveness, a type of energy and power in which the physical and the spiritual are inseparable and which is demonstrated in the capacity to give comfort—a word that, of course, implies strength. I see love in the sense of an overflowing and all embracing warmth that admits no barriers. And I see that these human qualities, which those who manifest them most would often see least in themselves, are universal. This is true of you and me. Those others can see it in us, as we can see it in them.

We have to learn tenderness towards ourselves. Not the

tenderness of self-indulgence, which, since it degrades us, is cruelty, but tenderness and respect for our true identity as a manifestation of God's will. Unfortunately we have also all developed a false sense of identity. It is a patchwork of the things we would like to be, or fear we are not; the qualities we would like to think we possess, or fear we don't; our actual achievements and our fantasies; our feelings of inadequacy, and the like. But this is the surface, the persona, the mask whose grimace covers the divine ground of our being; both Eckhart and Ruysbroeck actually affirm in identical words that 'we are God in God'.

Yet how little, even among Quakers, is this identity stressed. Even we, I sometimes think, state it as a dogma we profess to believe but do not really *feel* to be true. Perhaps all dogmas become empty word forms. Or perhaps we develop a false sort of humility. The realisation of the truth should, of course, make us humble, not however because we are Pascal's refuse of the universe, but for the very opposite reason. The combination of humility and triumphant pride in our divine identity is beautifully expressed by Angelus Silesius:

> I am the image of God: therefore if God could see
> Himself, he must look down and see himself in me.

Even so, how do we know it's true? 'The Light Within', as Rufus Jones says, echoing many others, '... is an experience'.* It is something we must feel, but perhaps we do not always recognise that we are feeling it. It may come with a dramatic and unmistakable intensity. Or it may come as a slow widening of consciousness of which we are as little aware as we were, when

---

* Rufus M. Jones, *An Interpretation of Quakerism*. London: Quaker Home Service, 1930, rptd 1979. Here one of the best known Quaker writers expresses a widely held belief of Friends.

young, of growing taller; but this widening may suffuse our whole lives with new conviction and purpose. The experience is commonly encountered in meeting for worship, but it may come at any time. The strength of the experience waxes and wanes. Sometimes we may forget about it for days on end, but if we look back over a period of time we see that there has been a change; we have grown. The false identity is weaker. The fantasies of material achievement, the selfish ambitions, the *amour propre* are less evident as we come into closer contact with the real self. We are happier in a different way, but we are also unhappier because we see it is necessary to abandon illusions to which we are still attached—and we see how many of them there are. What is happening to us, in Ruysbroeck's words, is this: 'God in the depths of us receives God who comes to us; it is God contemplating God'.

It is perhaps only fair, after speaking in this rather general and abstract fashion, that I should illustrate what I am discussing by recounting my own experience. Almost all my life, before and after joining Friends, I had been interested in religion, especially mysticism, but it was largely an intellectual interest; not something that touched my heart. Then, about twelve years ago, a period of strain and some danger came to a sudden end. For several days thereafter I experienced a lightness and happiness so intense that I can only call it bliss. I had no visions, however; nothing startling happened, but I came out of it with a firm conviction that I must look to my inner life. What had been a scholarly diversion must become real. Since then there have been plenty of lapses and blind alleys, but nevertheless I can look back with some astonishment at the sort of things I did and wanted in the past.

We must learn to love ourselves. Not to pamper, but also not to berate or belittle—that would be disparaging God's handi-work. Indeed to love ourselves rightly is the precondition of loving anyone else. Meister Eckhart puts it like this: 'As long as you love another person less than you love yourself, you will not really succeed in loving yourself; if you love all alike, including yourself, you will love them as one person that is both God and man'.

In a way it sounds easy. All we need is love, as the Beatles rightly used to sing. But most of us are steeped in wrong ideas about ourselves. There is much we have to unlearn before we can accept the simple, life-giving truths. In some respects, in fact, the habits of human existence load the dice against us. We have somehow forgotten who we are; and this is the source of all our errors. From our earliest years we are filled with false ideas about ourselves, swallowing the degrading theories of some theologians or behaviourists or straightforward cynics about our natures. And as we are wretchedly convinced of our badness, we compensate with grandiose boasts about our virtue and cleverness. Forgetting the source of all goodness and power in the splendid nature that we share in, we claim personal credit for every excellence, every demonstration of our individual superiority (and, by implication, someone else's inferiority). Thus the Light is hidden, the truth forgotten, the Seed enclosed in a husk.

But the Light, the truth and the Seed are intact; being in and of creation, they cannot be destroyed. They are the real self and they shine through everything. Despite all the difficulties and obstacles, love irradiates our lives.

We must nevertheless strive for awareness, to keep awake and conscious of our essence, to be watchful. But during so much of our lives we sleep, oblivious to Blake's trenchant call:

'Awake, awake, O sleeper of the land of shadows, wake! Expand!'

Instead, we believe that the dreams of our false selves are the reality. We are also asleep in another sense. We are not conscious of who we are, but behave like automata responding to stimuli. The wisps of consciousness, that we mistake for mind, flicker around the past with guilt, nostalgia or regret, or the future with hope or apprehension. We are not, to borrow from the telling title of a pamphlet by Douglas Steere, present where we are. But we don't recognise the fact, as is illustrated by a good story about St Francis. The saint and a fellow traveller were discussing prayer. The latter claimed that prayer was easy. St Francis said it wasn't. Why? Because it's difficult to remain recollected, to be conscious of the prayer as one is saying the words. The man said he had no such problem. All right, said St Francis, if you can say the Lord's Prayer and honestly maintain that you have been conscious throughout, knowing what you were saying and not parroting the words—then I'll give you my donkey. The man answered: Great, the donkey is as good as mine; and began to pray: 'Our Father, who art in heaven, hallowed be thy name, thy . . . and will you give me the saddle as well?'

This tendency to sleep is the common human condition, but it is not natural. That is to say, it is not according to our nature. We only have to recognise that nature, the Holy Spirit, the Christ, the 'that of God' who never sleeps. Only? To do so is the basic purpose of all religions, but the purity of this purpose has been distorted and obscured. It takes a George Fox to restore the radical simplicity of religion, a simplicity Friends have always striven also to reflect in the conduct of their lives.

We often strive too hard. Obsessed with the sense of our imperfection, we struggle with our temptations, struggle to pray, struggle to remember God. But this is the wrong way. Since we are made in God's image and likeness, have God within us, we already *are* perfect; we only have to recognise the fact in quietness and gratitude. Also we have all the knowledge we need, since our inner selves have access to, indeed form part of the infinite understanding of God. The deeper level of our mind is the universal mind, the source of all wisdom. However, our access to the deep mind is blocked by a rubble of prejudices, fears, memories of hurt, confusion, humiliation, by likes and dislikes, and above all by misinformation about our nature. We are under the illusion that we can solve all our problems, including our spiritual ones, by an effort of the intelligence. So we push and shove, dredging up our opinions and fixed ideas, gobbets of information and theory, whereas all we need is to be still, to listen and to allow for the operation of grace.

I am not disparaging the potential of our experience and education to help us towards the truth, but only when they serve as a channel for the operation of the universal mind. Of ourselves, using only our acquired skills, we can do nothing. A Friend, Mary F. Smith,* wrote aptly that praying about her work meant, firstly 'to realise my own inability to do even the familiar job, as it truly should be done, unless I am in touch with eternity, unless I do it "unto God", unless I have the Father with me'.

The mind, the truly human mind, connects us with the universal intelligence. (The Tibetan Book of the Great Liberation refers to mind as being of intuitive wisdom, the sole seed, the potentiality for truth, the Buddha essence, and the All-Foundation.) It is not the mind of the computer with its vast data bank of material and theoretical information, its muscle memory, its autonomic action that maintains our vital functions. These may be closely linked and the computer may serve the eternal mind. If, however, we think that the computer is in control, we lose sight of the real mind.

---

* Mary F. Smith, 'The place of prayer in life' in *Studies in Quaker thought and practice*, ed. by Gerald Hibbert. London: Friends Home Service Committee, Pt. 2, 2nd edn., 1936.

The real mind might be compared to a clear, deep pool. You can look down and down and never see the bottom. But the leaves of a nearby tree fall and cover the surface, so that only a pattern of leaves is visible (a different pattern of leaves for each person with their various 'identities', quirks, oddities, experiences, ideas, culture, notions, isms). You might never know, unless you had seen it earlier, that the pool was there at all. But sometimes a wind comes, a breath of reality, that disturbs the leaves and reveals part of the pool, and on very rare occasions the leaves are permanently blown away.

The leaves on the pool, those blobs on the mind, the frills, conceits, vanities and fears, have nothing to do with our true nature. But they obscure it, creating the mirage of illusions within which we so largely exist.

The most lethal of these illusions are false ideas of our own nature; that we are stupid, inadequate, wicked; or conversely that we are clever, charming, generous—which is just as bad so long as we think it is to our credit rather than God's.

Then we identify ourselves with our bodies. *I* am well. *I* am ill. *I* have a headache—which soon becomes *I am* a headache; the throbbing pain possesses me. But I am not my body. I am heir to all creation and my body is a temporary construction of celestial ideas for my habitation.

Yet again we identify ourselves with our work, or role, or function(s) in life. Most women, happily, have ceased to identify themselves as their husband's wife, but most would also still identify themselves as teacher, doctor, member of parliament, mother, housewife, or whatever. And I would have identified myself as professor, or whatever I was at the time. But although I worked in that capacity *I* was not a professor any more than *I* was a husband, father, ratepayer, owner of a driving licence, etc, etc.

No. We are not our roles. However important or splendid

they may be, we are something more sublime: a self, described thus by Thomas Traherne in his poem *My Spirit*:

> O wondrous Self! O Sphere of Light
> O sphere of Joy most fair;
> O Act, O Power infinit;
> O Subtile and unbounded Air!
> O living Orb of Light!
> Thou which within me art, yet Me! Thou Ey,
> And Temple of this whole Infinitie!

It stands to reason that we must also see others in the light of that of God within both them and us. As we view ourselves, so must we view them—indeed, as I have suggested, it may be easier to see in them the divine essence. If we are not to blame ourselves, we must be even more scrupulous about criticising others to whose inner struggles we cannot be privy. All we know is that they, as we, do have those struggles; they may be manifested differently, but they are basically the same—in criticising them we criticise ourselves and so do wrong to both. Most importantly, as we love ourselves, so we must love them. (I am told by a rabbinical scholar that the injunction to love our neighbours as ourselves means to love them because they are as, that is the same as, ourselves.)

By the same token, we cannot flatter our friends, telling them, for example, that they are cleverer, wiser, or kinder than so and so. We cannot give to an individual credit for something for which s/he is not responsible; this is taking from God what is properly his, and may be the inner meaning of the commandment concerning theft. What we can do, however, and seldom do sufficiently, is to praise in our friends the manifestation of divine qualities; love, intelligence, strength, courage, steadfastness, loyalty, sweetness, generosity, unselfishness. In a sense this is an act of worship in which divine and human love are wonderfully blended. It is also an act of service to our friends which helps them to recognise the nobility of their state and so to realise it more richly. The more we are able to treat people in this way, the more wealth of diversity shall we find in them. At each meeting we will discover something rare and wonderful, a new prism refracting the infinite radiance of eternity.

I have been speaking of an attitude towards ourselves and an attitude towards others, but this is somewhat paradoxical. What determines these attitudes is what we have in common: that of God. This is not just a figure of speech. Although we are all distinct human beings, there is a level at which we all come together, re-joined in a shared dimension of being that has been recognised by many and given different names—Jung, for example, called it the collective unconscious. Howard Brinton expresses it like this: 'The deepest self is that which we share with all others. This is the vine of which we are all branches, the life of God on which our individual lives are based'. This, indeed, is virtually a paraphrase of Traherne: the mystics see things alike. The achievement of unity, within oneself, with God, and through God with others is the aim of the religious life; one might say, the purpose of all human existence. To the extent that we achieve it, we are in constant touch with and deeply influence each other, even if we are often unaware of the fact. Should anyone doubt this, they may consider how greatly we are affected by an atmosphere of happiness, or one of depression. This common and not particularly spiritual level no doubt accounts for such phenomena as telepathy and the wordless communication that often occurs between people who are close to each other. I have sometimes experienced it in meeting for worship, when my thoughts have unexpectedly turned towards some topic upon which a Friend speaks shortly after. A not particularly religious friend once told me how, oddly enough in a taxi in Calcutta, he suddenly felt a sense of complete identity, first with his fellow passengers, and then with everyone else in the world. He could no longer feel hostile to Richard Nixon, he said, it being the time of the Watergate scandal, because in a sense he *was* Nixon.

All this may sound far-fetched to those who have not had a comparable experience; others will recognise it. It may appear trivial or insignificant, as when one day a bus conductor answered all my questions before I had asked them; it may be overwhelming as in the case of Pascal who, articulate as he was, could only describe it by the one word: 'fire'. These are all experiences of union at one level or another, and it is to some form of union that mysticism and contemplation lead us. The author of *The Cloud of Unknowing* called it 'a one-ing exercise'. This one-ing is impeded by our false identities. To Buddhists the myth, as they see it, of separation brought about by these identities, is the ultimate sin. Hell is the state of apartness.*

When we get below or beyond our persona we glimpse a universality in which we all merge and the you-me distinction is dissolved. This is not to say we lose consciousness of individuality. The mysterious paradox is that we see ourselves both as distinct and as part of a whole from which we came, to which we shall return, and in which we have our being. Our consciousness is enlarged and seems to incorporate many other conscious-

---

* I am much indebted to William Johnston for the insights gained from his *The Inner Eye of Love* (see bibliography). This book, together with Bede Griffiths's *Return to the Centre* (also mentioned in the bibliography) together constitute one of the most powerful arguments in the interminable debate about universalism and whether, or not, Quakerism is Christian. These two authors are both Catholic priests, Christian theologians of impeccable credentials, but they have a profound respect for the spiritual qualities of Hinduism and Zen, which for them illuminates aspects of their own belief, just as Christianity enriches the Eastern religions.

nesses, so that we are able to perceive reality with something far fuller and stronger than our human senses. Remember the deep, clear pool that is mind. It rises from a limitless subterranean reservoir into which we can all plunge and in which the fantasy of separation is drowned. Experiencing this in some measure, we begin to develop a real understanding of our relationship to each other, not just our friends, but everyone. We are all members of one body, as St Paul tells us so cogently. If one is hurt, all suffer, just as my whole body seems to suffer, although the rest is unharmed, if I sprain my finger. We live in a world in which more than half the human beings are hurt by hunger, poverty, oppression, ignorance, or war. It is as though more than half our body were scorched, damaged by far more than a sprain: must we not all share this pain and try to alleviate it? We are involved with all humankind because we *are* all humankind.

A frequent response to this kind of statement is despairing: 'it's all very well to say that, and it may be true in some sort of metaphysical and theoretical way, but what does it really mean for me; what can *I* do?'

The answer is simple, although the implied principle may sometimes be hard to follow. The more we recognise and acknowledge that of God within ourselves, thus enjoying that communion which is the essence of prayer, the greater will be our access to the knowledge that will show us what to do. And the more we recognise God in others, the closer we shall grow to them. Eventually, hardly realising we are doing so, we shall wisely, tenderly and suitably minister to each other, serving by the same token both God and each other. And an important part of our ministration is making peace, with which the rest of this work is concerned.

III

CONCEPTS AND PROCESS IN
PEACE MAKING*

This chapter marks a change of gear. The first two dealt with what might be termed a spiritual psychology. This one and the next two are concerned with the application of that psychology to peace making. The present chapter begins with definitions and/or discussion of peace and related subjects. This is important because the study of peace, unlike, say, economics and still less like a natural science such as physics, is new and inexact. It lacks a generally accepted vocabulary and clearly defined basic concepts. It is therefore necessary for anyone writing on these subjects to clarify the meaning assigned to various key terms. Words like peace, conflict and violence are commonly used in ordinary conversation, but if we wish to use them as, in a sense, technical words with more precise meanings, these have to be explained. In truth words like peace are particularly difficult, being emotive, abstract and subjective. Many of the disagreements that arise in argument about peace are, in fact, semantic. People use different words when they mean the same thing; or the same words when they mean different things. The difficulty is perhaps compounded because the people who have contributed to the study of peace and conflict (the two are often bracketed) have come from every possible background of experience and academic training; the founding father of the subject was a

---

* Anyone who wishes to explore further the concepts in this chapter might wish to glance at my books in which some of them are developed at greater length. These are: *Making Peace*. London: Tavistock, 1971, and *Mystics and Militants*. London: Tavistock, 1972.

Quaker, Lewis Fry Richardson, a statistician who was elected to the Royal Society for his pioneering work in meteorology.

It will be obvious to the reader that my definitions and interpretations are greatly influenced by my own views of our nature. I don't make this explicit at every point, but I hope the relationship between the spiritual idea and the peace concept will be clear. Some might object that this is not 'value-free' social science (or whatever I am writing). In my opinion, there is no such thing. All economists, anthropologists, historians, etc, however honestly they deal with data, are also expressing a point of view. The only real dishonesty is to pretend that one is not doing so.

Peace
This is the most crucial as well as the most difficult of words. When I was first actively involved in a situation of international conflict it never occurred to me to doubt that peace was simply the opposite to war, and vice versa. It was only when I began to try to think systematically about this experience that I realised what I had in fact always known, but for a mind set about the words 'peace' and 'war'. This is that there are countless human situations that could never be called peaceful, yet in which there is no war or overt violence. These situations exist on the large scale and the small. In whole societies the poor, or those who have the wrong coloured skin, or religion, or language suffer as a result. The suffering is economic, cultural, political, social and psychological. I began to see that, albeit with all sorts of exceptions, whole systems like colonialism do violence to the underdogs. I recognised that in far too many parts of the world superficial order is maintained by the ruthless extirpation of dissent, and that the manifestation of anguish and desperation is suppressed only for fear of reprisals. In such places the killings, terrorisation, torturing and detention without trial are justified as

necessary to maintain 'law and order'. The surface, to the casual visitor, is calm, 'the trains run on time'. But is it peace? Clearly not; almost all the horrors of war are enacted, almost all the suffering endured. I do not at this stage wish to get into the question of the counter-violence, the frantic revenge of the victim, that is engendered by such oppression (and termed terrorism by the rulers). I would only wish to emphasise that the absence of war is a necessary, but not a sufficient, basis for defining peace.

In his Swarthmore Lecture of 1974, Wolf Mendl mentioned that the word we translate into English as peace has various quite different emphases in different cultures—the Will of God, Justice, Prosperity, Tranquillity of Mind. I think that many of us in this country would, if pressed, define peace as meaning, apart from the absence of war, the absence of conflict (a complex word that we shall discuss shortly) and that we would equate this with the maintenance of a fair, decent and democratic social order—coupled with reasonable restraints for those who wantonly attempted to disrupt it. But others would lay much more emphasis on correcting what they would consider to be injustices and inequalities (another concept we will soon examine). Some members of minority groups, people who have felt the powerlessness of poverty, handicap, or age would say that the 'peace' of the majority is purchased at the cost of the misery of the minority. It is not my aim to argue whether this opinion is or is not correct, although I know of many instances where it certainly is, and that it is held, and held passionately, by many, because to them peace can only be achieved by changing society. For them peace means a society that does not do violence to its members. I should perhaps add that this view of peace, which might be termed the revolutionary view of peace, is by no means confined to this country. It forms a part of the philosophy of many groups struggling against oppression throughout the world. Because it usually involves struggle and confrontation it might be called an 'unpeaceful' approach to peace. Much of the sadly bitter and angry controversy that rages among those concerned with the study of peace reflects the conflict between those who believe that peace cannot be achieved without radical changes, and those who maintain that this approach is the antithesis to peace, and that we must build upon whatever stability and goodwill exists in society.

There are also those who would define peace much more subjectively. Although most of us would probably include contentment in our private definition, there are some who would strongly emphasise, as do Indian and Confucian culture, tranquillity and peace of mind. Some, indeed, would identify peace of mind as the peace of God. It is, of course, obvious that there is some relationship between inner and outer peace. If we are frantic, angry, frightened, troubled, we behave correspondingly. If we are inwardly quiet (of course I don't mean apathetic, impassive or torpid) we are much more likely to act with discrimination, justly, positively, and peacefully.

However, in searching for a definition of peace that would be operationally useful for tackling unpeacefulness, I found it very hard to take account of all these very different dimensions: the inner or subjective, the revolutionary change, the preservation of stability. Above all, I found that the word peace was used by all its various interpreters abstractly, to indicate a *condition*. The more I considered it, however, the more I became convinced that although there were obviously countless conditions that we might, or might not according to inclination, call peace, *they almost all arose out of what we human beings do to each other.* (I say almost, because the peace of God clearly comes from God; even so, the experience of this peace must have an enormous effect on how we behave towards our fellows.)

Consequently, I found it helpful to define peace as a relationship—between individuals, groups, nations, races, etc—rather than a state or condition. I first defined the character or the relationship negatively. Considering all the relationships which by virtually any standard would be deemed unpeaceful it seemed that they have one thing in common—they do damage to people. By being killed, maimed, treated unjustly, oppressed, exploited, cheated, manipulated, by having their minds distorted by propaganda or falsehood, by being derided, humiliated, corrupted, enslaved, terrified, driven from their homes, forced to cringe and beg, made to feel foolish or inferior, their chance of actualising their real human potential is sadly diminished. Some, I know, triumph in adversity, but I have seen enough misery to know that they are few. Moreover, we have to think of those who perpetrate the damage. They are as much maimed, although differently, as their victims.

Such, then, are unpeaceful relationships. They range in magnitude from the global relationships between the wealthy nations and the poor ones to the subtle—and often apparently decorous—persecutions of family life.

Peaceful relations, by contrast, are those in which, through the structure of the relationship, the individuals or groups involved have a greater opportunity, and are indeed actively helped, to become what they really are.

Some Friends may feel that I have offered an interpretation of the Peace Testimony that has moved too far from its original, and indeed rightly continuing, character as a testimony against war, which is certainly the epitome of unpeaceful relations. They may further feel that by extending the concept of peace and unpeace, in the sense of peaceful and unpeaceful relations, I have spread it so widely as to be meaningless and impractical; surely, they may complain, the scope of my study, covers almost the whole range of human situations. Yes, it does. I believe that the practice of peace making is, or should be, a universal human function. Springing from that of God within it is our common task to work for harmony wherever we are, to strive to bring together whatever is sundered by fear, ignorance, hatred, resentment, injustice or any of those conditions or attitudes of mind that separate us. I shall in general be concentrating on larger and more dramatic issues, but if the principles and practices appropriate to them cannot be applied on the smaller scale, there must be something wrong with the principles.

I hope, also, that what I am saying will be of encouragement to those people, of whom I meet so many, who do not see what they can do to alleviate the miseries of the world. But the great issues are built on a foundation of countless smaller ones. Every time we sow love where there was hatred we readjust the balance of the cosmos.

Conflict, Violence and Other Concepts

There are several other words and concepts associated with peace, negatively and positively. These include conflict and conflict resolution, violence in its various forms, non-violence, confrontation, reconciliation, and awareness.

Conflict is sometimes taken as the antithesis of peace, but this is not entirely correct. The inaccuracy perhaps arises from two different ways in which the word is used. We sometimes employ it as a synonym for a fight, a struggle, or a battle; sometimes as meaning an incompatibility, or conflict of interest. If used in the second sense, the word need not necessarily imply anything destructive, although of course a conflict of interest may lead to a conflict of the first sort. It may, however, mean a creative difference of opinion out of which enlightenment may grow.

The word confrontation is also often considered in conjunction with conflict—a confrontation may lead to conflict (in the sense of fight) or vice versa. But it need not be always so. A confrontation may bring into the open a festering conflict, such as existed in America between Blacks and Whites. The angry confrontations of the late 1960s, although often frightening, in fact led to a far greater understanding by many white Americans of the underlying conflict, and consequently to improved race relations.

The related concept of conflict resolution may apply to one of two categories of situation. In the first, which is perhaps how it is usually understood, two conflicting parties of approximately equal power, either face to face or through intermediaries, work out mutually acceptable compromises, bargains and concessions—or try to do so. In the second, the two hostile groups are unequal in power, one being possibly a deprived minority. In this case there is little point in the sort of negotiation carried out by equal protagonists; why, after all, should the stronger party bother to compromise? The conflict is, therefore, to be resolved in a different way. The stronger may seek to do so by completely crushing the weaker. Or they may be more subtle and try to reduce tension through reforms that alter conditions superficially, but are merely temporary palliatives for discontent, since they do not touch the basic injustices. Or, thirdly, the underdogs may decide to bring the conflict into the open and to resolve it by attempting to remove the inequalities that caused it. These three last types of conflict resolution are likely to lead to unpeaceful relationships, open or concealed. Only if the underdogs use the methods of non-violent action (to be considered later) can this be avoided.

Much, perhaps most, unpeacefulness and both sorts of conflict have to do with inequality and injustice. This fact has uncomfortable implications that the would be peace maker must face: most injustices are committed by those who have more power upon those who have less. This in itself constitutes an unpeaceful relationship and anyone who wished to change it would incur the displeasure of the powerful. Nevertheless, it is important to remember that injustice and equality do not always coincide. Certain sorts of equality could be unjust—to those, for example, who had dangerous or taxing work, or greater responsibilities, but who were paid the same as everyone else. By the same token, inequality does not necessarily mean injustice. Many roles in life, such as parent and child, teacher and student, high ranking official and ordinary citizen, show considerable inequalities of power. However, although this power may be abused, it is not necessarily exercised to the disadvantage of the less powerful.

Faced with injustice, many individuals and groups have resorted to violence, and violence must always be repugnant. The roots from which the word is derived imply the illegitimate or excessive use of force, and its effects are at the core of unpeacefulness, in the sense of damaging the fulfilment of our potential. On the other hand, we must recognise the dreadful and long drawn out suffering that has impelled people to resort to violence; the combination of desperation and idealism that has led them to follow this course and the reluctance with which they often do so. We should also remember that double standards are easily-applied to violence. Thus people advocate, as a means of reducing crimes of violence, the reintroduction of capital punishment or of flogging!

Both violence and conflicts of either sort have much to do with power. The under dogs are violent because, since they lack power, the top dogs have been able to impose upon them intolerable conditions; and because through violence they hope to gain sufficient power to change those conditions. This leads to conflict in the sense of struggle; and arises out of conflict of interest, it being in the interest of the rulers to maintain the status quo and of the ruled to change it. Sometimes it is mainly the violence of the victim, eventually taking up arms after fruitless petititions and appeals, that attracts attention. Everything was peaceful before, people say (meaning the under dogs were passive); why couldn't they (the oppressed) just be patient? But there *was* violence before, of the sort termed structural violence by Johan Galtung.* This term refers to the political and economic inequalities which are built into the social structure. The violence of the system deprives those at the lower end of the socio-economic scale of what is necessary to fulfilment, both materially and, since they are made to feel inferior and insecure, psychologically. They need not be directly harmed, but in most places where adequate statistics exist, because health is related to diet, hygiene and medical services, the poor and deprived have a lower life expectancy, and a higher rate of child and maternal mortality than the rich.

This is certainly true in Britain, although many people are unaware of the details.† It is startling to compare the life cycles of persons born into the higher socio-economic groups with those born into the lower. They have a four times better chance of surviving the first month of life. They are seven times less likely to leave school early. Consequently they are much more likely to go on to university and get a degree which makes them more than 20 times as likely as someone with GCE or similar qualifications to earn a salary that places them among the 10% of the population who possess about 90% of the wealth of the

---

* Johan Galtung, although even now only 50, is widely recognised as the 'father of peace studies' (which perhaps makes Richardson the grandfather). I am intellectually much indebted to him, having assimilated so many of his ideas that I cannot adequately acknowledge them. He has written a number of books, but I think the most illuminating of his publications are the papers he wrote for the Chair in Conflict and Peace Research of the University of Oslo in the 1970s (see bibliography).
† The statistics in this paragraph are taken from *Unequal Britain: a report of the cycle of inequality* by Frank Field. London: Arrow Books, 1974.

country. They will also be healthier, for the incidence of all diseases, except diseases of the eyes, is related to social and economic class. When they grow up and set up home, they are four times as likely to own their own house. If they go into industry, they are much more likely to go into management, in which case they are 16 times less likely to be booked or clocked in and 22 times less likely to be penalised for lateness. And the higher they rise an increasingly large proportion of their income will be in the form of fringe benefits, many untaxed. They are 11 times less likely to be out of work. Finally, to complete this cycle of injustice and inequality, because of their relatively pleasant and comfortable lives, their children will have longer lives than the children of the less fortunate. The mortality rate for unskilled workers is, in fact, double that for professional people. Moreover, these disparities have continued, proportionately unchanged, since at least before World War One, before which adequate statistics are not available. This is what is meant by structural violence.

There is probably an element of structural violence in all societies. This is often virtually unrecognised, except by those who suffer most flagrantly from it—gypsies, gay people, women. We need not be violent people, liking to inflict pain on others, to operate the violence of the system; we are simply conditioned not to see it, or if we do, to feel we cannot change it.

Friends must, of course, always reject the use of violence as a means of making peace—apart from everything else, the logical inconsistency is glaring. Many will rightly advocate negotiation and the political process at local, national, and international levels. This, especially in effective democratic systems, is both possible and desirable. I hope that some of what I shall say will be applicable to it. I am concerned, however, with cases in which negotiation or political activity of a more formal type, is inappropriate or has failed.

One alternative is the course of non-violent action. The greatest exponents in our era have been Mahatma Gandhi, Martin Luther King, Dom Helder Camara, Cesar Chavez, Daniel Berrigan and others, including many Friends, who added spirituality to political astuteness. The essence of non-violent action is to combine a political and social militancy in effecting the desired changes in society with a concerned attempt to bring about a change of heart; to convert those whom they are opposing. These have to be confronted. Life has to be made difficult for them by massive strikes or civil disobedience. But the aim is not to destroy, to seek revenge, or to humiliate. It is that all should be reconciled in a new and regenerated society. I should make it quite clear that this approach to non-violence is quite different from non-violence adopted as an expedient tactic which, except for the use of physical force, is the psychological and ideological equivalent of war. Such was the civilian resistance by the Norwegians against the Nazi invaders during World War Two.

Reconciliation is, of course, the ultimate aim of peace making. It is a word of power and beauty which implies, etymologically, the re-establishment of a council; as though there had once been a council of humankind that had been fractured by our errors and ill-doings. Many feel that all the impediments to peace can be removed by reconciliation. Others think, however, that the correction of injustices is sufficient. The latter believe that the reconcilers are impractical idealists; the former, that those who seek justice first will fail through not recognising the primacy of spiritual issues. I believe that we should always consider peace making in terms of the long-term goal of reconciliation, but that we should recognise the existence of intermediate goals—the proper resolution of conflict and the removal of injustices—without which reconciliation will be perhaps impossible to achieve.

Finally, I should like to consider a concept, that of awareness, that is central both to a discussion of peace making and to the philosophy which, for me at least, underlies it. By awareness (and comparable terms such as consciousness, watchfulness and the state of being awake) I mean essentially awareness of our own nature as partakers of the divine essence. This awareness is constantly lost in the shifting focus of thoughts, ideas, associations and the like. The more constantly we maintain it, however, the greater our understanding and the greater our capacity to act as peace makers and reconcilers.

But our level of awareness or consciousness of self (I use this phrase because self-consciousness has other connotations) is the measure of our awareness of others. If our sense of self is clouded, we see others through a haze that distorts them also. We are then less able to perceive external reality.

Awareness at all levels is linked, but for our purposes there are two important dimensions. If we do not have a measure of self-awareness, we can see nothing with clarity. On the other hand, perception of social situations, of conflicts of interest, of structural violence, depends not only on a measure of self-awareness, but also of information. Certainly most people now know much more than they did a few years ago about conflicts affecting, for example, the Third World, women, immigrants, or homosexuals, without having greater self awareness—they are simply informed by the media. The point I wish to make is that without greater self-awareness, we do not *feel* differently and so do not *act* differently. If we see things in the same way, we behave about them in the same way. But to the extent that our perception of externals is related to a deeper vision of our own natures, so will our actions be changed.

Thus awareness is the root of all change. Moreover, since peace means a change from unpeaceful to peaceful relations, it is the very source of peace.

The Process of Peace Making

In this final part of the chapter, I shall try to put together in a brief discussion of the process of peace making some of the ideas we have just considered. This is the process in which, of course, the peace maker applies his peace making skills. Now, however, we are only considering the process; the application is the subject of the next two chapters.

Like everything else, peace making combines yin and yang, inner and outer, public and private. When the two are out of harmony so that yang predominates, the peace maker depends on manipulating external conditions, political manoeuvering, alternating threats and promises, the subtleties of bargain and compromise. This is the mode of a Kissinger or Metternich. It may effect the settlement of a particular dispute, but seldom establishes the deep harmony of reconciliation; it may merely eliminate the symptoms of unpeacefulness without removing their cause.

When people emphasise the yin, they are attempting to change feelings and attitudes. They rely on protest, persuasion or moral pressure rather than on negotiation, political analysis or diplomacy. They usually have little impact on events.

When yin and yang are harmonised, peace makers are 'as wise as serpents and as harmless as doves'; politically astute and realistic, but with a humanity wide enough to include, if they represent the victims of oppression, those they oppose. They strive for lasting peace among all contestants.

I trust that my introduction of the Chinese concept of yin and yang will not be considered fanciful or irrelevant. According to tradition, yin represents what is gentle, tender, loving, co-operative, sensitive, caring, subjective, intuitive, lunar, dark, feminine, imaginative, mystical. Yang represents what is strong, efficient, objective, rational, bright, solar, competitive, male, practical. When the two are in proper balance, as they are in mature individuals or communities, harmony reigns. When separate, their qualities become distorted, exaggerated, weakened or malign. Strength becomes ruthlessness, sensitivity becomes frailty, the maleness or femaleness become sexism— and so on. It seems to me that the most typical Quaker lives combine the yin and yang very effectively in a blend of the mystical with the practical and sensible. I believe most people would accept that these two interwoven and mutually support-ing strands do exist in Quakerism, whatever we may call them, and are also highly relevant to peace making. I prefer, but not fanatically, to speak of yin and yang because it is satisfying to find yet another relevance for a rich and ancient idea.

It may be recalled that I define unpeacefulness as the damage we do to each other's potentiality for realisation. It is mani-fested in many ways. It may take the covert form of emotional wounding, or the crudely physical hurt inflicted in war (which also inflicts psychic harm). It may consist of the complex com-bination of cultural, psychological and economic deprivation inflicted by colonialism, or in general by the rich and powerful on the poor and weak. It exists when two hostile parties—which may be individuals or states—compete for the same indivisible prize. It exists when people are impelled by pain (usually of un-recognised origin) or by fantasies and illusions (often rooted in a mythical past) to vengeful conflict. It is the product of every sort of exploitation, oppression and manipulation, whether between sexes, classes, races, religions, communities, tribes, ideologies or nations. It is the fruit of every ism.

No cases of unpeacefulness are identical, but there are certain typical patterns requiring different approaches to peace making.

One of the commonest is the relationship between the strong and the weak, when the strong abuse their power. There are, of course, many such relationships, some open and flagrant, some disguised. The most intractable are those in which the under dogs have a limited understanding of their condition. 'The rich have always exploited the poor', I have heard it said. 'But it's the will of God and there is nothing we can do.' And some would add: 'It's not really so bad; we might be worse off'. Here hopelessness and ignorance are reinforced by fear of what might be done to protesters. Situations of this sort can never alter until their victims come to perceive them differently. I term those the Stage of Quiescence.

The first step, therefore, must be a widening of awareness. I am not now suggesting who should attempt this, or how, merely that it is necessary.

Once awareness has grown, the quality of the relationship is no longer accepted. Those who have been damaged by it, seek to change it. If they ever imagined that complaint would suffice, they will soon be disillusioned, for it is in the interest of the powerful to keep things as they are. The poor soon realise that they must struggle if they are to better their condition. But they are very weak. Their first efforts, therefore, are to gain sufficient power to enforce change. This is at the root of most revolutions.

Peace makers at this stage, which I refer to as the Stage of Revolution, are, in fact, revolutionaries. This is a word which arouses hostility in many, although it means fundamentally a turning around, hopefully from violence to peace. 'You are advocating conflict rather than peace' people protest. But this shows a defect in understanding. The unpeacefulness was already there, the strong were already afflicting the weak, and if the weak bore their lot with a tortured grin it was because they were frightened, uncomprehending, without hope. If the victims, eventually, become violent it is not, of course, peaceful, but some would see the revolution as a necessary step towards ultimate peace.

Revolution, like peace making, involves yin and yang. In what most people would consider a typical revolution, an armed and desperate struggle, yang predominates. People are killed and degraded, including many who have nothing to do with the issue. Some would excuse this as an evil necessary for the final triumph of good. Others would say that violence always breeds violence and that the end result, whatever the purpose, is merely to raise the level of violence throughout the world. In such outward revolutions one party, if successful, overthrows another. Then, all too often, there is simply an exchange of tyrannies.

But revolutions may be peaceful (evolution some might say) as many in this country. When yin and yang are in balance the outward change occurs, but is complemented by an inner change of awareness that stabilises peace. How does this happen? There is no box of magic tricks, no entirely relevant university course. The peace maker is not only a person of wide experience skilled in strategy, but a compassionate teacher and servant who has dedicated her/his life—literally, since s/he must sometimes be prepared to die—to peace. Such, of course, is the non-violent approach of a Gandhi.

It must be stressed that this sort of revolution may be, if necessary, no less tough and militant than that dominated by yang. After mass political mobilisation, every type of pressure is brought to bear against the government, the economy, communications. The aim, however, is not to destroy or to repay violence in kind. It is to undo an oppressive system, but not those who operate it. A fine distinction, perhaps, but a powerful one: the difference is between hatred and love, between vindictive triumph and compassion for the confusion of discomforted rulers. The final aim is to convert them, so that they may participate in building a just and peaceful society. It would be one in which the human rights of all were recognised, including the right to be spared both the humiliation of oppression and the degradation of oppressing.

The role of revolutionary peace makers is difficult and dangerous. If, as is inevitable, they represent the oppressed or are of them, they will arouse vicious hostility from those in power and from fanatics of all colouring. They can certainly expect persecution and quite possibly assassination. Moreover, their resolute refusal to play the demagogue or stir up hatred will make them suspect among their own people. They must be clever, daring and well informed. At the same time they must renounce the conventional use of these qualities to glorify themselves or their cause, and to attack, belittle or deride their opponents. They cannot tread this path unstumbling unless inwardly quiet and harmonious, passionate in faith yet dispassionate in action. They can have no thought of revenge, but must love their enemies and seek eventual reconciliation with them.

We haven't considered yet what might be thought of as the peace maker's main role of mediator or negotiator. Here is the reason. In the unpeaceful relationships between the strong and the powerless it is often pointless for the peace maker to urge the strong to mend their ways. This would be an approach in which yin predominated, but why should the strong respond? It is to their advantage to maintain the status quo (this, of course, is why there has been such resistance to change in Southern Africa, in Iran, in much of Latin America and in all too many other places).

When the struggle is between more or less equals the role of the peace maker is very different. S/he is very properly a go-between, an honest broker, an arbitrator.

Publicly, this involves seeking face-saving formulae for those inclined to make concessions, compromises enabling both sides to edge towards agreement, bargains that may be struck and the opening up of indirect channels of communication. These peace makers need both general and specialised knowledge. They must understand the political, economic, social or strategic elements of the situation and have a good grasp of underlying theory. They must be sensitive to the constants of conflict situations (between individuals—as in marriage—or groups, or nations, or ideological blocks). These include fear of appearing weak, the need to neutralise the opposition and to maintain public morale, to encourage allies and supporters and to elicit international (or at any rate wider) support. In addition peace makers must master the intricate details of a specific situation. This is the yang aspect.

The private aspect of peace making, the yin, involves creating the psychological atmosphere in which the public work can be carried out with some hope of success—and this in fact applies in every type of unpeaceful situation. This is essential because in all conflicts the judgement of those who have to make decisions, however capable they may be, is warped in some degree by their fear, anger, resentment, ambition, vanity, anxieties and feeling of impotence. I have sometimes thought that if the greatest diplomatic and military minds of history were to offer their solutions to, say, the problems of Northern Ireland or the Middle East, they would be rejected. The actors in such conflicts see them through a haze of desperate feelings. Only when this is dispersed can they properly evaluate them. It is a crucial part of balanced peace making to blow away the haze. But the peace makers themselves are in a similar situation. They carry around within themselves the legacy of the past, the fears for the future, and the pressure of the present which interact to impair their discrimination. They cannot help others to be free of this determinism until their liberation from illusion about themselves has begun. 'O peace maker', said Hazrat Inayat Khan, 'before trying to make peace throughout the world, first make peace within yourself.'

My own work began largely at the yang, the public, level. I

have, however, become increasingly aware of the importance of the less understood private level of peace making. For this reason the following chapters deal more with the yin than the yang, which is in general better known and well documented. But of course the two modes must always be in balance. When this is not so, there is inevitable distortion and the peace making process will be impaired and incomplete.

In conclusion, I should point out another difference between public and private peace making; one that does not necessarily, although this is often the case, correspond to the contrast between yin and yang. Some peace makers, in the sense of intermediaries or those who advocate a particular type of solution, represent an external power—a state or an economic interest. Their main concern is to serve that power rather than those between whom they are trying to make peace. They may even be prepared to use the strength of their masters to enforce solutions that may not be in the interests of all involved.*

The peace makers whose private status rests on their independence of an external force are concerned, by contrast, with the suffering of all the people caught up in the conflict. The price paid for this independence is the lack of means to put pressure, to lean heavily on the contestants. No stick and carrot technique can be applied. On the other hand, their weakness is also

---

* I should draw attention to a useful differentiation, which I follow in practice although I do not use the terminology, between 'settlement' and 'resolution' of conflict. Dr John W. Burton and his colleagues of the Centre for the Analysis of Conflict define the former as an arrangement, possibly unsatisfactory to both contestants, imposed by a third party; the latter as a mutually acceptable accord reached by the parties in concord and leading to a peaceful relationship—reconciliation, in fact. I need hardly emphasise that Quaker peace makers, although third parties, are *never* in a position, even if they so desired, to impose 'settlements'.

their strength. It resides in the trust and confidence they may be able to inspire because of their impartial goodwill.

The following table aims to set out schematically the different types of unpeaceful relations and the various approaches to peace making that we have just been considering.

UNPEACEFUL (VIOLENT) RELATIONSHIPS

	Between the Weak and the Strong		Between Equals
Yin/Yang Function	Stage of Quiescence. The under dogs suffer oppression, but without clear comprehension or hope of change.	Stage of Revolution following change in awareness. The under dogs struggle for power to enforce change.	Reciprocal violence resulting from rivalry, conflict of interest and faulty perceptions.
Yang predominates	Occasional aimless violence	Violent revolution aiming to over-throw rulers and dismantle system	Political negotia-tion, diplomatic measures, arm-twisting, threats and promises, bargaining. Aim: settlement of conflict.
Yin predominates	Passive discontent	Protest aiming to change the attitude of the rulers	Persuasion and propaganda. Aim: convince contestants of undesirability of conflict.
Yin and Yang in balance	Growth of awareness and beginnings of organisation	Non-violent revolution aiming to change system and, eventually, to win over previous rulers, involving them in reconstruction	Political and diplomatic moves for peace, coupled with efforts to clarify perceptions of decision makers. Aim: reconciliation.

IV

THE PRACTICE OF PEACE MAKING (1)

The task of the peace maker has two dimensions. The first is to transform unpeaceful into peaceful relations. The second is to work for conditions conducive to peace and unfavourable to violence. I am grateful to Walter Martin for pointing out to me that these dimensions reflect the spirit of the two declarations by George Fox out of which, through various shifts in emphasis, today's Quaker Peace Testimony has developed.

These are, of course, firstly to the Commonwealth Commissioners in 1651, in which he told them: 'I lived in the virtue of that life and power that took away the occasion of all wars and I knew from whence all wars did rise, from the lust, according to James's doctrine'. (In his reference to the Epistle of St James, George Fox, as usual, gets down to fundamentals. It is perhaps worth reminding ourselves of James's words at the beginning of Chapter Four. 'From whence come wars and fightings among you? Come they not hence, even of your lusts that war in your members? Ye lust, and have not: ye kill and desire to have, and cannot obtain: ye fight and war, yet ye have not, because ye ask not. Ye ask, and receive not, because ye ask amiss, that ye may consume it upon your lusts'. These words are as appropriate today as when they were written, for most of the ills that plague us arise from acquisitive greed, especially when institutionalised in oppressive political or economic systems.)

The second declaration, made to Charles II in 1661, stated: 'We utterly deny all outward wars and strife and fightings with outward weapons, for any end or under any pretence whatsoever', and continued that 'the spirit of Christ, which leads us into all Truth, will never move us to fight and war against any man with outward weapons, neither for the kingdom of Christ, nor for the kingdoms of this world'.

This declaration is the clearest possible renunciation of war as a means of solving human problems. If, therefore, we take action to resolve an unpeaceful situation, it must be non-violent. The spirit of this declaration lies behind much of the work I have been involved with for years in attempting to promote peaceful ends to violent struggles.

The first declaration extends the concept of peace making beyond the righting of wrongs, the healing of breaches, or the making up of quarrels. It is to do with change, and at two main levels. Firstly, it may be manifested as change in the feelings and outlook of individuals. These may come to live in 'the virtue of that life, that [takes] away the occasion of all wars' together with, as I think we may interpret George Fox, all selfish, greedy and destructive behaviour. Or secondly, it may be brought about in social situations and institutions (again through non-violent practices), altering what was exploitative or oppressive into something nurturing human growth and the fulfilment of potential.

In this chapter and the next I shall try to suggest how Friends and other like-minded people who reject violence might act today on these ancient principles to preserve or make peace, or to create and maintain conditions conducive to peace. In general I shall be discussing the human elements in peace making—the establishment of relationships, the deepening of contact, the improvement of communications, the growth of awareness, positive attitudes towards those who oppose us. All these should be viewed in the context of our previous consideration of human nature. I shall not be much concerned with the specifics of negotiation, the bargaining and the compromises. The details vary greatly from case to case, while the general principles are well known to the student of conflict theory or labour relations.

54

Moreover, the non-official peace maker, in the international field at least, seldom has the power to negotiate. His or her role is more to help create favourable conditions for negotiation.

The need for change is implicit, if not explicit, in much that I say about the level of awareness, perception of reality, attitudes, social systems, economic and political institutions etc. There is scope for another, and perhaps longer, Swarthmore Lecture on building a society better geared to the uses of peace, and I would stress that the many people who are working to humanise social institutions and practices are indispensable peace makers. However, even if I were capable of discussing this type of peace making (peace building might be better) it would take me away from my main theme. I can only suggest that anything that emphasises the fulfilment of human potential, and sharing and cooperation, as through community development, must be furthering the cause of peace. Likewise, to follow self-interest regardless of others—whether individuals, communities, or states—is to act unpeacefully: institutions based upon this principle are intrinsically violent. But of course the details vary greatly according to culture, tradition and social settings.

I should make it clear, however, that in presenting ideas about the practice of peace making, I am not suggesting that it is at all easy, or that there is any set of gimmicks or magical solutions. On the contrary, it is very hard. The process of peace making is hardly ever simple and is seldom brought to a complete conclusion. The more complex the situation, and the greater number of interlocking elements—economic, political, historical and so on—the more difficult it is to achieve peace. It is unusual, moreover, for everyone involved to agree to the terms of a settlement. An angry, dissenting minority that feels its interests to have been improperly represented may easily bring again to boiling point the cauldron of strife. There is, moreover, a more fundamental difficulty. Human affairs are most intricately inter-

55

connected, and there are few isolated conflicts. It is impossible to separate them neatly from each other, resolving their problems piecemeal. Yet this is not necessarily bad, for although the unpeacefulness of one situation may flow over into another, so may the peacefulness.

Whatever the difficulties of peace making, however, it is an integral human activity. It is taken to restore harmony in one corner of a universe whose very existence perfectly demonstrates balance and harmony. Frequently a particular peace making effort seems to have been completely unsuccessful or at least to have had no ascertainable effect, but we must act in faith. No one can assess the impact of genuine peace making, undertaken with love. The ripples may spread throughout eternity.

Before discussing peace making in specific types of unpeaceful relationships (see Table on page 52), we should consider the universal principles that follow from the belief in that of God in everyone. These concern our relationships with all people in the situation—with our associates as well as with those who oppose our efforts, with all the protagonists, with oppressors and their victims, the rich and the poor, the powerless and the powerful, the violent and the meek, friends and foes, and with ourselves. Without a relationship of trust and acceptance nothing good can be achieved; violence or deceit will rule.

Acknowledging God in All

The first and enduring principle is that peace makers must look to that of God in every one. Their awareness of the divinity within each human being will help each to act in accordance with it. This is the true basis of peace making. The *acknowledgement* of the good in others promotes the *expression* of the good. The alternative is to manipulate, arrange or persuade, even to threaten, which is clearly out of accord with the Quaker approach to making peace. But unpeacefulness can only be really healed through those involved in the situation acting in accordance with God's will, that is to say, manifesting the Christ within. We can help by recognising and giving thanks for this great force. In saying this I am not advocating passivity or quietism. On the contrary, the peace maker will probably be very active, but if the source and guide of the activity is the real self, good must flow from it. Conversely, if action is based on the illusion that the isolated, separate human being is the mover, only confusion will follow.

Listening and Attention

The principle just outlined is abstract and universal. A second derives from it, but is more concrete, concerning the development of relations with others through the attention with which we listen to them and care for them.

I must again begin with our relations with ourselves, for these depend on our relations with others. This needs little explanation: if we are happy, those around us are more likely to be happy, but if we are gloomy and self-centred, we can't expect to spread joy.

The most essential preliminary to peace making is prayer, or meditation, or whatever is the more suitable term. I mean that purposeful stillness in which we sink through the turbulence and the scum of the surface—the anxieties, isms, and preoccupations—to the eternal, the Light of Christ within, through which we are joined to the eternal Christ. Thus we are also joined to those other individualisations of the will of God whom we are privileged to be about to meet. Thus, by the same token, we can draw on the wisdom of the eternal and universal mind.

Through prayer we must also eradicate fear—of making fools of ourselves, of making mistakes, of being hurt; fear creates the very things we dread. It is a plague. It comes from lack of love, for perfect love casts it out. It comes from not recognising our true nature, for nothing can harm that of God within us which *is* us, or Atman, or Al-Haqq, or the Buddha nature, or however any culture expresses the universal verity. As Shankara said: 'Why should a man have the slightest fear if he knows that he is the self, the inner and the outer, beyond birth, decay, old age, and death?' (But he added: 'Whenever a man sees the slightest difference between himself and the infinite Brahman, fear will arise in him'). And the psalmist sang 'The Lord is my light and salvation; whom shall I fear? The Lord is the strength of my life; of whom shall I be afraid?' When we are proceeding to the encounter it is important to think freshly about what is to happen. If we brood about the last meeting, the quirks and un-reasonableness of the people we are about to meet, it is more than likely that we will behave in such a way as to evoke those very things. We should go with the pleasurable anticipation of meeting a child of God who will reflect the infinite glories of his creation. Then, even if it is someone we know well, we will see new and wonderful qualities hitherto concealed by the blinkers of our presumptions. There is an important corollary to this. We must never, as we have been commanded by Jesus, make judge-ments on people. Not only are the judgements false, for each person is a reflection of God, but in making them we increase that person's difficulty in recognising his/her true nature. And tell a child often enough that it is stupid and so, superficially, it will become; and we might as well be thrown into the sea with a mill-stone hung around our necks.

The absolute necessity for attentive listening was borne in on me very early in my experience of peace making. I became aware that what my friends and I were trying to say was often not heard, especially at the start of a meeting or if the situation were particularly tense. A question or observation would, it is true, be answered, but not responded to in any meaningful way.

It was as though our words were filtered through a compound of anger, fear, resentment and preconception that radically changed their meaning. It was to this new meaning that the people we were talking with responded, often angrily and usually irrelevantly. Because of the general circumstances, what we said was often perceived as having a threatening or insulting meaning, or a perfectly straightforward question would be taken as a criticism. During the Nigerian civil war, for example, the federal government were extraordinarily sensitive to the harsh judgements of the world's press, and the most innocent enquiry about some aspect of the war would be seen as hostile. We, in fact, were not being listened to, but if we had responded with irritation, it would mean that we, too, had not been listening. We assumed without question that the way to overcome these difficulties of communication was to say very little, certainly not to argue, re-explain or contradict, but to be inwardly still and as receptive as possible. This would usually enable the storm of emotion, so natural in men under great pressure, to blow itself out. Listening, however, does not come easily to us. We are obsessed by the noise of our own thoughts and can hardly wait until the other person has stopped talking before making our own little speech—which we have been too busy composing to hear what the other said. Recall almost any party or committee meeting.

I have also always found that things were likely to go very wrong if I carried my judgements over into a meeting. Once or twice I have gone to an important discussion tainted by negative emotions, feeling perhaps superior to the men I was going to see because they had been involved with great violence. If, as happened on occasion, I had seen the awful effects of this, feelings of revulsion, outrage and condemnation would be added. However polished and diplomatic the manner might be, these feelings somehow pervade the atmosphere. I had to learn, therefore, to dissolve them. It was totally unfair, I realised, to direct them at people whom I knew to be at least as much moved by suffering as I was and who, at the headquarters, could do little to influence the details of what happened at the front. In fact to get rid of my distress by projecting it on to others was a form of self-indulgence. This is not, of course, a condonation of violence, but a denial of our right to make judgements on those who are implicated with it.

To listen deeply means many things. Firstly, we must prevent our mind from wandering (telling phrase) and hear exactly what is said. Then we must listen to the tone of the voice: if you ask me how I am and I answer dolefully, shoulders sagging, that I am fine, you get the right answer: but not from my actual words. There may, moreover, be even subtler emanations that you can pick up. And there is yet more to listening. Paradoxically, the most informative listening is not concentrated solely on the person to whom the attention is given. The hearing is opened wide with that person at the centre, but with other sounds such as passing traffic not excluded. No filtering mechanism is employed, such as we may have to use when trying to hold a conversation in a noisy room, but which reduces general sensitivity.

Our civilisation is altogether too loud to encourage accurate hearing. Most Africans are much more generous with their attention, but the best listeners I have met are the Native Americans. In several tribes, listening is an art specially taught to children. When my Native American friends visited me they would always fall silent, Quaker-like, and listen. How else, they asked, could they discover my condition and so speak to it, as they always did most effectively.

To listen attentively is to act autonomously. The listener has escaped the determinism of the automatic part of our nature operating through what I have termed the computer. To listen is, so to speak, to switch off or at least turn down the computer. Thus, as in prayer, so in listening we reach a deeper and more genuine part of our being.

Moreover, listening does not only lead to hearing and understanding, but also to speech. If we learn to listen, we will often find that the right words are given to us. These do not come as a result of careful thought, but spring directly from our more profound sources of knowledge. Although often very simple, their effect may be powerful. I remember being told of a much respected older Quaker whose ministry was always very brief. One day at meeting for worship, he stood up and simply said: 'God is love', and all who heard him were moved in their very depths. Another could have used the same words, but if they had come from a different level of his/her being, they would have had no more effect than many other phrases that have become cliches. Jesus also instructed his disciples, saying: 'take no thought beforehand what ye shall speak, neither do ye premeditate: but whatsoever shall be given you in that hour, that speak ye: for it is not ye that speak, but the Holy Ghost'. Thus to listen is to listen also to God, and what we are given to speak as a result comes from God.

The importance of listening, then, is that we not only 'hear' the other in a profound sense but communicate with him or her through our true nature. This in turn evokes a response from the true part of her or his nature. For this reason very strong and positive feelings are often aroused in the listener and the listened to. This is why peace makers should learn to listen as attentively and as constantly as possible. They not only discover what may be vital to know, but they reach the *part of the other person that is really able to make peace, both inwardly and outwardly.*

I recall one dramatic incident. I had to visit the headquarters of a guerilla leader in circumstances that were potentially dangerous. I was apprehensive, realising that if I was unable to establish rapport with him, he would probably suspect me and become hostile. I knew I must prepare myself well and, when I arrived, to listen intently. At first he was cold and watchful. Suddenly he smiled, ordered refreshment and said 'people don't usually come to see me looking happy and relaxed'. We became friends and were able to explore ways of finding humane rather than violent solutions to the situations he was involved in.

As a relationship develops into friendship, there is much that we can do for each other; and nothing is more important than to keep in the forefront of awareness the real being, the Living Light of Christ, in each of us. On this basis we can assure our friends of their strength, wisdom, courage and goodness—for these are the qualities of God in which we share. The more deeply we are conscious of these priceless possessions, the more effective our peace making.

(In all this I may seem to be appealing to faith and, indeed, here is a question I have often debated with myself. I believe in the Christ within, but is my belief strong enough to move even the smallest molehill?—Lord, help thou mine unbelief. However, it has come to me that genuine belief is knowledge rather than faith in something for which there is no proof. This is the knowledge that comes through the deeper self and the universal mind to which we there have access. What I have just been saying, therefore, I state as fact rather than problematic belief.)

Encouragement of those with whom we are engaged in seeking peace does not mean giving blanket approval for everything they do. On the contrary, if they act in a way that is contrary to their true natures, the fact should not be ignored. Nor should they be told it doesn't matter, although the pain that perhaps impelled them to behave in a particular way should be treated with sympathy. But constructive criticism should be offered in the spirit of an Indian legend that appeals to me. A snake that had been converted by a holy man, had promised never to bite another human being. But the villagers took advantage of this and attacked it with sticks and stones. The snake, angry and disillusioned, complained to the guru, who answered: 'but I never told you not to hiss'. We have an obligation to 'hiss' at the right time.

It is perhaps worth repeating that the development of human (as opposed to machine-like or automatic) relations to other human beings applies to all types of unpeaceful relations. It applies to both those who are working with us and those who are working against us. The specific application of the principle will obviously vary according to circumstances; we speak in one way to a close friend, in another to a relative stranger, in yet a third way to someone who feels hostility or suspicion towards us. But there is no need for this to cause concern. The right words will come if we are inwardly prepared. Indeed, the peace maker should always be ready. Apart from the practical skills that can be easily learned, the first and last responsibility is to bear in mind and to act upon the principles of George Fox's epistle of 1652. 'Stand still in that which is pure, after ye see yourselves; and then mercy comes in. After thou seest thy thoughts, and the temptations, do not think, but submit; and then power comes. Stand still in that which shows and discovers; and then doth strength immediately come. And stand still in the Light, and submit to it, and the other will be hush'd and gone; and then content comes.'

Earning Acceptance

The third principle is that peace makers must earn acceptance by those among whom they would work. They may be considerably helped by their reputation, as we were helped in India and Pakistan by the widespread knowledge that Friends had long worked in the sub-continent and been close to Gandhi. But this only facilitated the initial contacts; all individuals must themselves prove worthy of trust. For this it is necessary to be both tactful and consistent. The firm establishment of close human relationships depends upon the maintenance of unwavering goodwill, clear impartiality, and helpfulness—small services that Friends have been able to perform on peace making missions seem often to have contributed towards establishing their position. This position is strengthened if it is known that they have, solely in the interests of peace and for no possible personal advantage, exposed themselves to discomfort, exhaustion, and perhaps danger. This was tellingly illustrated by an incident early in the civil war in Nigeria, a country in which Friends were not very well known. We had suggested to the then head of state that there might be some point in a small Friends delegation visiting Biafra, then under a state of siege. He did not believe that this would be helpful and added that we should be flying on an 'illegal rebel plane' which his forces had instructions to try to shoot down. When we said we were prepared to take that risk, he said he hoped we would visit him again—if we returned. We did so a few weeks later, after complex and difficult journeys, and were cordially received. He said that there had been no mention of our trip on the Biafran radio, which meant that we had not used the occasion for any personal publicity and that the Biafrans also presumably hoped to use us as a channel for communication, implying that they were interested in negotiations. This was the beginning of a good relationship that lasted throughout the war.

Nevertheless, a relationship with two hostile parties is not easy to sustain. Even after initial suspicion—'we don't understand how you can claim to be friendly with us, who are gentle, peace-loving people, as well as our enemies, who are treacherous war criminals'—is allayed, there may still be squalls. This was shown by another incident during the Nigerian hostilities at a

stage which we had gained a considerable measure of confidence from both sides. Friends in America issued a fund-
raising advertisement which, under the title (so far as I recall) of
'two peep holes into hell' showed horrific pictures of Biafra and
Vietnam. The Friends responsible understood little of the quasi-
diplomatic activities which were going on, but the Nigerian
Federal Government were very offended. 'We thought you were
our friends' they said. Fortunately, the relationship had a solid
foundation and no lasting harm was done, but for a little while
the atmosphere was very highly charged. It is important to
remember that people who are fighting each other are very tense,
and in consequence unreasonably touchy.

All this may take time, and those engaged on these missions
have often feared that they were wasting their efforts going the
rounds of people who do not always seem particularly keen to
see them.

Unofficial peace makers, such as Friends, have initially to
follow a different path from that of accredited diplomats. The
latter have a defined and accepted role, a ready-made position
and entrée into a number of circles. The former have to make
their own introductions or to rely on the good offices of others
similar to themselves, or who have had experience of Friends,
having perhaps attended one of the diplomats' seminars. Thereafter, however, the effectiveness of both groups depends to a
large extent upon the development of personal relationships.
This may prove easier for the unofficial peace makers, for it will
eventually be accepted that they serve no national or com-
mercial interests, but are working under concern for the relief of
human suffering. It is this concern that draws them to the scene
of tension or conflict, rarely if ever a direct invitation, and the
depth of concern that impels them to commit themselves to a
given issue may become their best credential. 'Where are our
silent friends?' asked one head of state, when the Quaker peace

making group had not been to see him for a while; he then sent for them and asked them to go on a particular mission.

This incident was a demonstration of trust, proof that a sound relationship had been established. Further evidence of trust is that the peace makers, instead of being at best tolerated messengers, are entrusted with sensitive and confidential tasks, become involved in issues of policy, and are asked advice. They may then also be able to exercise the traditional Quaker function of speaking truth to power. I think that to some Friends this suggests marching into the office of the president, the local mayor, or whosoever it may be, and issuing a ringing denunciation of his policies. If a relative stranger had done this to any of the presidents or prime ministers I have known, s/he might have been treated with cold courtesy or hot anger, but the message, because of the manner of the delivery, would have been unheard. But a peace maker who has won the right for his/her opinions to be heard may be able to 'hiss', to convey uncomfortable truths which, from many others, would have been too unpalatable to be listened to. I have been present when the Quaker group was able to make a strong case to the commander in chief that his military policy, far from frightening his foes into submission, was impelling them to desperate resistance—which of course led to further escalations. The Friends were not attempting to instruct the general on tactics, but on the psychological insights they had gleaned from visiting the other side. These showed that, despite the conventional military wisdom, measures that increased human suffering were counter-productive. I must point here to a difficult question: how much or what to tell? We have sometimes obtained information which might be significant for making peace and saving lives, but which could also perhaps be employed to win battles and serve a particular political cause. There is no easy answer. Each case, it seems to me, must be judged separately. All the more necessary, then, to keep burningly alive the first principle: the recognition of the divine in everyone.

Although I have mainly been referring to unofficial diplomacy at the international level, I hope that what I have said has some relevance to other types of diplomacy and to other situations, including those in our own country. In the latter instance, it should usually be much easier to make contacts, there being no major cultural differences and no extremes of tension. In the former, I believe that the general principles of establishing relationships are similar; the means of gaining trust are universal, however much difference there may be in context. Moreover, the difference between official and non-official is in many respects blurred. Although I have never served as an official diplomat (although in other respects I have held official positions) I have as an unofficial diplomat worked very closely with both national governments and international organisations.

Persistence

The Nigerian civil war was a conflict that, because of the horrifying starvation and the inaccessibility of the besieged rebel state, attracted an unusual amount of attention. A number of prominent people made well publicised trips to West Africa in the search for a settlement. Most of them were quite unable to achieve anything, however, and returned home after a few days. These efforts contrasted sharply with the unpublicised work of missionaries and others who remained for years to share the dangers, miseries and privations of the people to whom they were committed.

Similarly, peace makers who derive their impetus from a deep sense of kinship with all human beings, particularly those who suffer, must be resolutely persistent. One may judge the authenticity of their ideals by the strength of their refusal to give in to discouragement. Indeed, just when peace makers (and so probably everyone else) are most pessimistic about the prospects for peace and consider giving up, it is most important to plug on without losing heart.

When Friends who were searching for a solution to the Zimbabwe war had made a number of seemingly fruitless journeys, two of them visited a wise and much respected African leader. He urged them to continue their efforts, irrespective of their apparent lack of effect. 'You may not seem to be getting anywhere', he said, 'but at least you are keeping alive the idea of negotiation.'

Genuine peace making must continue as long as the need exists. The problems of unpeacefulness are not resolved until the ultimate reconciliation, which means that in some respects peace making is a life long vocation. We cannot resign from our involvement with the relief of suffering although circumstances such as age may lead to our manifesting it differently.

*　　　*　　　*

I feel it necessary to conclude this chapter by discussing a delicate issue which, if not universal, is nearly so—difficulties between peace makers and their friends. Let us consider a hypothetical situation based on my own experience in several places and augmented by what I have heard of places I have not been to.

There is a violent situation—a civil war, a liberation struggle, a bitter political conflict, or injustice and oppression that have not yet erupted into open violence, but are likely to. Local Friends are inevitably caught up in the situation, possibly facing an outcome in which they fear their lives may be adversely affected. They are, of course, against violence, but their own loyalties and affiliations are inevitably involved. What if violence is perpetrated by those protecting them from danger? They are faced with an agonising dilemma. Even in less extreme cases painful choices have to be made. Being a Quaker does not, of course, imply a particular political persuasion; in Britain there are Friends who vote for all the major political parties and it is pleasant that political difference does not predicate spiritual disunity. Nevertheless, controversy can arise in Friends Meetings over political issues—and in other churches also. I recall that great tension developed in the USA between those who upheld the dispatch by the American Friends Service Committee of medical supplies to North Vietnam during the war, and those who condemned it as a political act, illegal and so unQuakerly.

In the hypothetical violent situation, some Friends decide to take a specific line, perhaps to support the rebels, perhaps to side with the existing regime. They will certainly take it out of spiritual concern, but it will probably bring them into opposition against other members of the Meeting, who feel that their particular interests and points of view are misunderstood, not taken into account, or ignored. Strong feelings of anger and anxiety may be aroused in which political ideas and spiritual values then became inextricably interwoven.

If these Friends have come from outside the country the controversy is intensified—what is it to do with them? They don't understand the issues; they arrive with their ready-made opinions and bias against certain groups, which may indeed include many of the local Friends; they just stir things up and then go home leaving local Friends to cope with the consequences.

Having been such an intruder and knowing the feelings of those intruded upon, I can feel sympathy with both parties. Those who are impelled to take some positive action, whether insiders or outsiders, have a strong obligation to examine their motives and their premises very carefully. Are they acting self-righteously; do they understand the full implications of what they are planning; do they feel superior to those who disagree with them; do they realise why some disapprove their actions? If so, let them reconsider what they are doing, and why, submitting the answers to the ultimate arbitrament of prayer to ensure that all motives of self-aggrandisement and ego-satisfaction are eliminated.

But they should also not be ashamed of their impulses. Having sought the truth with humility and sincerity, they are bound to act in accordance with it. I once discussed this matter, in a difficult situation, with an African Friend. 'There is no question', he said. 'You must tell the truth.' He meant, I think, the truth that all human beings are one in God and that this oneness gives equal meaning and dignity to us all, and conditions all our behaviour towards each other. We must only remember that this truth applies equally to those who are opposed to what we are doing.

If, after the most careful consideration, we are convinced that we are doing right, we should continue, neither deflected by the disapproval of others, nor upset and antagonised by it. Instead, we should understand their feelings and try to explain our actions—to tell the truth, in fact, not harshly but with loving concern for those who have good reasons for finding it hard to accept.

V

THE PRACTICE OF PEACE MAKING (2)

I have suggested that there are three categories of unpeaceful relationships. This typology may provide clues as to how to deal with unpeacefulness. The categories are: relationships in which the protagonists are unequal in power and in which the less powerful are *either* relatively unaware of the full implications of their position (the Stage of Quiescence), *or* more aware of it and hence active in trying to change it (the Stage of Revolution); and relationships in which the protagonists are more or less equal in power, as might be nations competing for economic or territorial gain, or business rivals, or neighbours engaged in a dispute (Conflict between Equals).

These types overlap and intermingle and are only clear-cut in extreme cases. These would be marked, for the Stage of Quiescence, by an ignorantly apathetic acceptance of the status quo; for the Stage of Revolution by a militant liberation struggle—and for the Conflict between Equals by hostility, but without oppression of one side by the other. The most difficult to distinguish are usually the first two, which frequently merge; there will be areas of awareness in the Stage of Quiescence and of unawareness in the Stage of Revolution. This may be illustrated by awareness of class (or socio-economic status) in Britain. At one level many people know a great deal about it, from badly paid workers to economists and sociologists; there has certainly been enough awareness to make a major impact on national politics. Moreover, most people have a general idea of class as something that gives them more, or fewer, advantages and makes them feel more, or less, comfortable in various settings—some, indeed, feel very angry about this. But very few have any exact appreciation of what the class of their parents implied for them, or what theirs—for the effects carry on—mean for their own children (see page 41).

Perhaps the most important single element is, in fact, awareness. Few human beings come into their full heritage of knowledge; the lack of a full measure of understanding always impairs action.

I have also suggested that an approach to peace making (or, I should perhaps say to at least changing a situation deemed unpeaceful) may be dominated by yin, or by yang, or may express them in a state of harmony. Because I take it as axiomatic that Quakerly peace making will always attempt to balance yin and yang, it is on this that I concentrate. Quakers are normally much too aware of spiritual realities, and of the danger of violence if they are neglected, to be satisfied with an approach stressing the yang; they are also too practical to over-emphasise the yin. This means that there are three appropriate types of peace making effort, one for each of the three types of unpeaceful relationships.

In writing these pages, I have been afraid of seeming abstract and remote, of separating ideas from facts. To speak of types of relationship or peace making may seem pedantically theoretical. I believe, however, that each one of us has been actively involved with the three main types of unpeaceful relationships and in several different roles—as the instigator of the unpeacefulness, as its victim, or in attempting to transform it into peacefulness. We are primarily concerned here with the last role, but it may help our understanding if we also remember the other parts we have played.

The Stage of Quiescence

We have probably all been involved in this stage. In it people are adversely affected by situations they may hardly understand and

72

certainly do not grasp fully, or which have implications they do not realise. Consequently they suffer dumbly, without hope or comprehension. These situations occur throughout the world and in every type and level of society. Their most extreme forms are usually associated with poverty and ignorance on the part of an under group and oppressive power on the part of rulers; but they are far from unknown among the humbler citizens of wealthy democracies. The most extreme example within my experience was in a remote and feudal principality in the Hindu Kush. Here the peasants, known as the Faqir Mishkin, literally the miserably poor, were not only subjected to forced labour by the rulers, but were taxed in kind, giving up one-tenth of the exiguous crops they were able to raise in the high and stony valleys. Every year, because of this tithe, they had used up their food supply before the new crop was ripe. Their chief diet during this period of annual semi-famine was grass seasoned with salt. The old and the weak died of hunger, but I was told that the most common cause of death was stomach blockage caused by the diet of grass. My wife and I were there at this time of hunger and the people were anguished that they could offer us no hospitality—the poorest so often have the most generous hearts. They feared and hated their overlords, but they accepted their lot without question. 'What can we do?' they said. 'It has always been thus. It is hard to bear, but it is our fate.' They had no hope, no idea of such concepts as social justice and human rights. The new philosophies of Russia and China, not so many miles across the mountains, had never filtered in.

My own experience of being a victim who was both ignorant and powerless (I was later a victim when I knew how to resist) was during most of my school days. I accepted a system that I feared and hated, having no inkling that I could in any way alter it or handle myself better, as I now see that I could have done. This was, of course, as nothing compared with what so many millions have endured, but it made a very strong impression on me.

As a perpetrator of unpeaceful relations I would single out my role as a father and a teacher. The fact that in both roles I have tried to act with love and fairness is irrelevant. I can see that I imposed my whims, predelictions and prejudices upon my children at an age when it was hard for them to express reasoned opposition and in fact were likely to accept them, however tiresome, as representing reality. They could only agree with what might have been highly unreasonable, or respond with tantrums, sulks or stifled resentment. I am profoundly touched that they are now so charming and affectionate to me.

As a teacher, at least until the experiences I referred to (see page 23) I imposed standards that I now see to have been conventional, artificial and inimical to real learning. I now realise that, although some of my students (I hope) liked me personally, they rightly objected to the system for which I then stood. But they could not see how the system could be changed, and so discontentedly conformed, afraid that protest would damage their academic prospects. And there may be other examples that I am too blind to see.

My experience as a would-be peace maker in the Stage of Quiescence, has been limited. In the late 1940s I worked with two rural communities in England. My task, as I saw it, was to help them understand their relationship with the authorities and so to act in such a way as would persuade those authorities to behave more tolerantly and sensibly. My efforts were fairly successful, but then—as seldom in some other parts of the world—the authorities were basically sympathetic. During several years as adviser on education and social affairs to the Government of Pakistan (which then included what is now Bangladesh) I had many opportunities to work on similar relationships. The results were varied. Although the authorities were seldom actually unsympathetic, the distance between them and the rural population was infinitely greater than in Britain. I can say little about how I carried out my work in these circumstances. I was not yet a Friend, and many of the ideas on which this book is based were foreign to me. I simply mention this period as illustrating a fundamental type of unpeaceful relationship with which I have personally striven.

I have, however, also been involved with groups of students, colleagues, friends, Friends, in efforts to raise our collective awareness. Although this may in some sense be desired, it is also very often resisted—it will reveal, we dimly feel, uncomfortable truths, it will prod us towards action that may be emotionally or even physically dangerous, it will disturb the cosy equilibrium of our lives. Attempts to heighten awareness, therefore, must not only take account of the intrinsic difficulties of conveying information, but also the reluctance or at least the ambivalence with which it is received. One approach to awareness-creation could be termed the shock method. The group is faced starkly, even brutally or angrily, with facts it would prefer to ignore. Thus in their angry confrontations with white liberals, the American Blacks compelled the whites to face up to their own racism. Or some of them. Others refused to acknowledge something presented so crudely. As they rejected awareness so their former patronage changed to hostility and complaints of 'ingratitude'. It is, literally in some cases, a hit or miss method.

A very different approach, which is particularly appropriate for small groups, is based on the assumption that people are much more likely to be able to accept displeasing reality if they are, in other respects, feeling secure. It is therefore helpful to establish an atmosphere of trust, interdependence and mutual appreciation in the group. People can the more readily explore together painful and potentially menacing awareness than they can do it on their own. In the whole process of peace making few things are more crucial than assistance in the perception of truth.

Cogent examples of the creation of awareness in the Stage of Quiescence are provided by the work of Danilo Dolci and Paulo Freire.* Many years ago, Dolci visited Sicily to carry out a short-term professional assignment. But he became deeply concerned over what he found there, and has remained ever since. Much has been written about his work by himself and others, so I shall only refer to one aspect of it that I have heard about from him personally. He was distressed that the rural people did nothing to resist the power of the Mafia, which dominated and exploited almost every aspect of their lives. Why, he asked, could they not work together and assert themselves? their corporate power would be hard to resist. They looked blank and answered that this was not their way. Dolci explained this by an example from the class room. When the teacher is frightening and domineering, the children are so concerned to keep in his good graces that they pay little attention to each other. All communications are between the individual child and the teacher; the links between the children are very tenuous. Dolci drew the following diagram

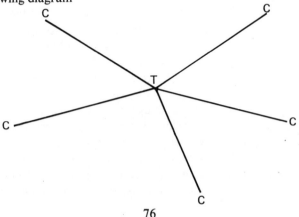

His aim, he said, was to change the pattern in the following way:

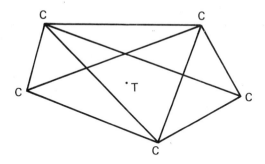

Here the teacher ceases to be the focal point of communication and the children are connected with each other—or, in the case in question, the peasants with each other, by-passing the Mafia boss.

Bit by bit, however, he was able to get the villagers to take part in small cooperative projects—building a chicken run, and a small dam; collective purchase of seed and feeding stuff. Slowly he was able to build up a pattern of collaboration and self-sufficiency in the community. The ability of the Mafia to control the community by its combination of menace, economic control and policy of divide and rule was greatly reduced. In view of his non-violent campaign for justice it is surprising to many that Danilo Dolci has not been assassinated—perhaps its very success and his consequent international reputation have rendered him immune.

Paulo Freire is a Brazilian educator and philosopher who at

---

* See bibliography. These two remarkable men, happily still with us, have written a number of other books the reader might wish to consult.

one stage worked among the desperately poor communities of North East Brazil. His task was adult education, but he found that available text books were not only technically useless, but confused and demeaned the students into the bargain. They had been composed for middle class children and spoke of such things as fathers who were lawyers and went to work in cars carrying briefcases, of flower gardens, costly food stuffs and so on. This was not only meaningless to adults living miserably below the poverty line, but also increased their hopelessness by hinting at a life that, however incomprehensible, they could never achieve. Like so many poor and oppressed peoples, they had no understanding of the forces oppressing them, and hence no hope of influencing, let alone changing those forces. (An American friend told me of a similar experience teaching literacy to young adults in prison; his texts were children's fairy stories.)

Freire decided that literacy could not be imparted outside a social context. If people learned to read and write about what mattered to them, they would learn easily and retain what they learned (the briefcases, grapes and flower gardens were forgotten as soon as learned). More importantly, he also believed that it was possible to learn these things in such a way that they imparted an understanding of the nature of their society and of the political and economic factors affecting it. This he did by a sensitive and ingenious system based on the use of words that his own researches showed to be of the greatest significance to the peasants. (He speaks of 'generative themes', the underlying reality of the peoples' existence; and uses the dramatic phrase 'to name the world' implying that by acquiring the power to define reality, it is possible to change it). It is small wonder that the authorities felt threatened by this dawning social awareness, this new capacity of the people to analyse their situation coupled with the beginning of skills which would help them to take an informed part in affairs. It is not surprising that Friere was imprisoned and later forced to leave the country.

These two examples raise interesting and perhaps contro-versial questions. Both Dolci and Freire took action to raise the consciousness of oppressed and ignorant groups. Such action, if at all successful, is inevitably conducive to social change and not inconceivably to turmoil and even violence. But I refer the reader to what has already been considered (page 47). Do we take the risks that these men took? Or do we avoid action that might upset an already violent status quo for fear that the results could lead to an upheaval? I suppose there is no clear-cut answer. In some instances the possibility of large-scale violence seems to be high, but these are very often the cases where pro-tracted and brutal tyranny have made radical change most desirable. Recent events in Nicaragua provide a telling example. In such cases dare we reject the risk?

My own belief is that we must act to raise awareness, or support those who do so. But everything depends on the methods used, and I would suspect the passionate call to rise and break the chains of despotism as one that might merely add violence to violence. I have chosen to discuss Freire and Dolci because both are men of great spirituality who reject violent solutions. Danilo Dolci has often been referred to as the Sicilian Gandhi and although this is in some ways inaccurate, it is not in others. His whole struggle, like Gandhi's including fasting, is directed against systems and not the people who run the systems. When public meetings were banned, he defied the regulation, but the gatherings were set to useful work of benefit to all groups of the community. Both hold to the ultimate goal of reconciliation. Freire says this: 'Dehumanisation, which marks not only those whose humanity has been stolen, but also (though in a different way) those who have stolen it, is a *distortion* of the vocation of becoming more fully human ... in order for this struggle (against oppression) to have meaning, the oppressed must not, in seeking to regain their humanity . . . become in turn oppressors, but rather restorers of the humanity of both'.

How should Quakers or other like-minded would-be peace makers approach the question of raising awareness among the people with whom they are working? To assume their ignorance and to assume one's own capacity could be both presumptuous and dangerous. Few of us are entitled to attempt specifically to increase awareness. The Dolcis and Freires developed their insights and skills the hard way. However, although most people working with communities in the Stage of Quiescence are primarily involved with agriculture, health or education, this work cannot be done effectively without the growth of awareness, for the problems of agriculture, etc., are not only technical, but also social. Workers in these circumstances need considerable skill. Apart from the yin abilities of developing good human contacts they need the yang abilities in a high degree. They must be *good* teachers, engineers, agriculturalists, vets, public health doctors or nurses, social workers, low-cost housing experts, etc. They need to understand the culture, the political system, the economy. Preferably they need experience (although there must always be a first time when the experience is acquired); certainly they must have sensitivity.

Let's return briefly, in conclusion, to the issues of awareness. Workers, peace makers, must learn how to handle the increased awareness that may develop as an incidental result of their work—that is discussed in the following pages. However crucial awareness may be as a prerequisite for social change, its primary importance is as self-awareness, awareness of our real self or nature. To fight against this awareness, even passively to fail to encourage it, is to oppose the Holy Spirit. In whatever way Friends may perceive the social scene, this awareness essentially means awareness of that of God in every one: and who knows whither this awareness may lead us?

The Stage of Revolution

This stage may follow many years after the State of Quiescence, or it may overlap with it, emerging from it. Without question it is a perilous stage. Within it have been the majority of the 150 or so wars that have raged since 1945. Many contemporary or recent foci of violence have been of this sort: Zimbabwe, Nicaragua, Iran, the Middle East, Angola, Ethiopia are obvious examples that spring at once to mind. There are, of course, many more.

These struggles, however grimly they have turned out, originated in the quest for justice and release from oppression. I would like to preface the discussion of this painful and controversial stage, the cause of such bitter argument among those who seek the same ends by different means, with some quotations that place the issue in a true perspective. First, John Woolman: 'Oppression in the extreme appears terrible: but oppression in more refined appearances remains to be oppression; and where the smallest degree of it is cherished it grows stronger and more extensive. The labour for a perfect redemption from this spirit of oppression is the great business of the whole family of Jesus Christ in this world'.

The second quotation is from Konrad Braun's Swarthmore Lecture of 1950: 'those who want to establish the realm of peace and love must work for justice too, indeed for justice first. If we regard peace not as a negative and stagnant posture, the absence of war, but as a constructive and dynamic process, then social justice, international justice, and inter-racial justice are indispensable as impelling forces to carry it forward. If love is to regenerate and inspire social, international and inter-racial relations, justice must first promote that freedom of personality, without which there can be no love'.

Thirdly, succinctly and to the point, speaks the Prophet Mohammad: 'Free the captive if he is unjustly confined; help everyone who is oppressed'. Next, Jeremiah: 'practise justice: hold in check the oppressor'. Finally, I am reminded by Joseph Fletcher, an American theologian, that 'Love and justice are the same, for justice is love distributed, nothing else'.

I would like to make it clear that in speaking of the Stage of Revolution, I am not advocating it. It would be happier and easier for the world if those who commit the unjust acts of oppression experienced a change of heart. (This, indeed, is in part the objective of the non-violent approach.) I would maintain, however, that this stage is almost inevitable in some form when oppressed people are becoming awakened. We are no doubt fortunate in many parts of Western Europe that something comparable to the Stage of Revolution was experienced before the desperate tensions, anger and dreadful weapons of our age had developed—but we might be unwise to congratulate ourselves prematurely.

But the Stage of Revolution is with us, actual, or in embryo, in very many parts of the world. We must be ready for it. We must learn to strive for justice, peace and reconciliation indeed, to recognise how close they are to each other; consider again James: 'True justice is the harvest reaped by peacemakers' (*NEB*). We must labour to change the Stage of Revolution from being one of bloodshed and hatred to one of construction and love.

The role of the peace maker at this stage is complex and difficult. Whose side is s/he on? The natural tendency might well be to feel such sympathy with the oppressed group yearning for justice, that we cannot avoid revulsion at the oppressor. This, however, is contrary to the principles of peace making based on the hope of ultimate reconciliation. The injustice of inequality is to be opposed, but the people who appear responsible for it (but who may as individuals be hardly to blame) are not to be hated or treated as enemies: as Friere says, they too are maimed by what they are doing. Instead, they must be considered as actors in the total situation who must also be rescued from it.

This sort of impartiality is not easy to maintain or to convey to others. Indeed, some Quaker peace makers, disregarding the example of John Woolman who inspired loving respect among both slaves and slave-masters, although he championed the former and accepted hospitality from the latter, have felt it was impossible to carry out this difficult moral balancing act. They have then thrown in their lot completely with the oppressed revolutionaries. (I use the word revolutionary in the sense of one who is trying to effect radical change, but not necessarily by force of arms.) If they were to have contact with the oppressors, they say, they would forfeit the confidence of their friends among the victims—and, to boot, have no influence on the oppressors. I find it easy to sympathise with this view, and indeed have acted upon it.

I was once asked to go on a mission of 'reconciliation' in East Pakistan (now Bangladesh) where ruthless overlords from West Pakistan were laying waste a defenceless province that had made a bid for independence. I refused; reluctantly, because I knew and loved the people. I was certain, however, that the overlords would reject my pleas for leniency. I could merely suggest that it might be in their best interests not to utterly alienate their subjects (who were producers essential to the economy) by decimating them. The only reconciliation I could practise would be to reconcile the underdogs to their subjection, to an ignoble surrender. If, most unexpectedly, they had given in to my persuasions the unpeaceful situation that had occasioned the rather mild bid for freedom and the subsequent slaughter and devastation, would have been frozen. After a few years of muted misery, the overt violence would have flared again.

Nevertheless, I believe I was wrong. It seems to me in general to be right at least to try—however unpropitious the circumstances may seem to be—to maintain a relationship with both sides. On more than one occasion, moreover, I have found it perfectly possible, although often difficult. It has to be made quite clear, however, that to maintain contact with the oppressors neither condones their actions, nor weakens support for and commitment to the oppressed. During the Stage of Revolution the peace maker must side with the victims; their liberation is his chief purpose. But it is a purpose he can help to fulfil by communicating with the oppressors; and his secondary purpose, which is to free the oppressors from the degradation in which they are trapped, cannot be realised unless he has some contact with them.

Our belief in that of God in every one must deeply influence our approach to the Stage of Revolution. We cannot destroy or humiliate those whose policies of violence, direct or structural, we oppose. The only course open to us is non-violent action. This we may practice ourselves if we belong to the oppressed group, or teach to others if we do not—but in either case we must learn its principles. (Inevitably, the more actively we are involved in the non-violent struggle, the harder it will be to keep up any sort of relationship with the other side: this is a hazard that has to be accepted, but we may take some comfort from the warm relationships that many non-violent activists, Mahatma Gandhi and Martin Luther King in particular, kept with their opponents and, on occasion, their gaolers.)

The doctrine of non-violence is the doctrine of Jesus; 'Love your enemies, bless them that curse you, do good to them that hate you, and pray for them that despitefully use you and persecute you'; 'resist not evil, but overcome evil by good'. And of the Buddha: 'Hatred does not cease by hatred; hatred ceases only by love' and 'Let a man overcome anger by love and evil by good'. Gandhi, following them centuries later, claimed that 'Non-violence is the greatest and most active force in the world.

One cannot be passively non-violent ... One person who expresses *ahisma* in his life expresses a force superior to all the forces of brutality'. And again: 'Mankind has to get out of violence through non-violence. Hatred will be overcome only by love. Counter-hatred will only increase the surface as well as the depth of hatred ... The virtues of mercy, non-violence, love and truth (are to be) pitted against ruthlessness, violence, hatred and untruth'. I finally quote Martin Luther King. 'The non-violent approach does something for the hearts and minds of those committed to it. It gives them new self-respect. It calls up resources of strength and courage they did not know they had. Finally, *it stirs up the conscience of the opponents so that reconciliation becomes a reality.*' (My italics.)

No one can pretend that non-violence is easy. It goes against all conventional habits of mind to love our enemies, indeed to cease thinking of them *as* enemies, to separate bad actions from those who commit them, to dissolve resentment and resign the prospect of revenge in all-inclusive love. But attitudes of violence are simply bad habits superimposed on a mind that is eternal and universal. Thus, fundamentally, the doctrine of non-violence is more natural than the dismal teachings of vengeance and retribution.

The Stage of Revolution may develop in many ways. If it began non-violently it may become violent (this has been the tendency in Southern Africa). If it is successful, the new rulers may only perpetuate, albeit in a different form, the same inequalities perpetrated by their predecessors. If the oppressors are sufficiently shrewd and subtle they will attempt to buy off the revolutionaries with concessions that make no difference to the power ratio, but can be disguised as victories for the oppressed, who will then relax their pressure. Or the whole movement may be crushed.

It will be undoubtedly very hard to preserve a consistent

approach to peace making during these possible vicissitudes. Peace makers will be under great strain and certainly unpopular with many. They can only sustain themselves by complete certainty as to the objective, the actualisation of the full potential of all concerned, coupled with the conviction that if they are not thrown off balance by doubt, fear, or confusion—hard things to avoid in the circumstances—the way will be made clear.

During this exceptionally demanding, confusing and dangerous stage (Gandhi and King, to whom I have so often referred were both murdered) there are several peace making tasks. Firstly, instruction and practice in the arts of non-violent action: how to defy, protest, obstruct, confuse, disrupt without causing to the oppressors the damage they have inflicted on the oppressed; how to do so with a minimum of risk to themselves and their fellows; how to accept, if they are inevitable, the risk and anguish. (The elaboration of this task would take a book in itself.)

Secondly, actual involvement in the revolutionary peace making process—it is vain to tell people what to do if one does not share in the action.

Thirdly, concern for the other side expressed by efforts, wherever these are possible, to establish some form of potentially constructive contact.

I must admit that I am poorly qualified to write about the Stage of Revolution since I have only once, briefly and disastrously, been involved in a typical (if there is such a thing) struggle in which the weak were trying to oppose the strong. A couple of other situations in which I have been implicated had a few of the characteristics common to liberation struggles. Circumstances, however, precluded my assuming the roles I have just described.

Conflict Between Equals

The more generally understood role of the peace maker is to be an intermediary, negotiator, or go-between in international, industrial or other areas of conflict. Most of my direct experience has been in the first, twice in Africa, once in Asia, once much nearer home. This has lasted since 1965, although with intervals and at varying levels of intensity.

It is in many ways a simpler and less ambiguous job than that of peace maker in the stages of Quiescence and of Revolution, and the people who get sucked into mediation have often a different background. Workers in the Stage of Quiescence may initially consider their tasks as being, say, teaching or public health. Gradually they may discover that the boundaries of an apparently straightforward professional assignment are expanding. The same people may find themselves projected into the Stage of Revolution by the social changes for which they have been partly responsible. They may then have to decide whether or not to change their peace making roles. However, peace makers primarily involved with the Stage of Revolution, especially if nationals of the country involved, may have a different type of background. They may be lawyers, politicians, disillusioned officials or, again, teachers, social workers or doctors (these last three are ubiquitous where social change and peace making are concerned). Official mediators in international conflict are normally professional diplomats or people well versed in politics. (Within other spheres, such as industry, are mediators with a different range of qualifications and skills about which I know very little and so will say nothing.) Unofficial mediators, Quakers and those associated with them or doing comparable work, seem to have no predictable qualifications. A number of Quaker International Affairs Representatives or Quaker Representatives as they are coming to be called (the closest approach to Quaker ambassadors), or people engaged on special missions in times of conflict, have been academics who taught a variety of subjects. Others have been business men. Some were selected because they knew the area concerned; others because they had relevant experience elsewhere, or were felt to have a positive approach to the issues involved. My case is perhaps typical. My first assignment to a Quaker peace mission related to the Indo-Pakistan war of 1965. I was an academic who had specialised for some years on problems of Third World development. I had spent one period of nearly three years and two shorter ones, as I have mentioned, as adviser on social affairs to the Government of Pakistan. During this time I had seen much of the country and knew many of the leading figures, including the President. (When a student I had even met Indira Nehru, as she then was, but that didn't really count.) In addition, I had become extremely concerned with the adverse effects of conflict on the development that my colleagues and I had been trying to promote. I also found there was a great deal to learn. We were shuttling between Rawalpindi and Delhi, hoping that our discussions might in some small way contribute towards defusing a dangerous situation, and I found that my 'qualifications' needed to be considerably supplemented. I had to make myself as well informed as possible about the current situation and its background. I had to learn to appreciate how raw are the feelings of those involved in conflict, how careful one must be to avoid touching sensitive spots. If I were to make ignorant or ill-judged remarks, anything else I might say would be disregarded. I even had to learn something of the conventions of diplomatic conduct. No one, of course, expects Quakers to imitate the professionals. However, to depart markedly from the norm of conventional behaviour when visiting a minister or official is unwise; it may distract attention from what one has to convey.

But the differences that may exist, and perhaps should not exist, between different types of Quaker peace makers, are less important than the similarities. They all share the ultimate aim of facilitating peaceful relations, of eliminating the social, psychological and material conditions that lead to conflict, and of answering that of God in every one. In whatsoever sphere this may be carried out, it is a very different task from that of the pure technician whose job begins and ends with building an irrigation system or marketing a cash crop; or that of the revolutionary who aims to overthrow one government and replace it by another, and is not particular about the means; or that of a diplomat striving to bring a particular conflict to an end. There may be no such thing as a 'pure' technician, revolutionary or diplomat. I suspect that the objectives of most would extend beyond the specific job, but this would be a matter of degree. The peace makers I am speaking of are as much interested in eventual reconciliation as in the solution of immediate problems. They perceive everything they do in this dual context: its relevance to ultimate harmony among all concerned, and to the removal of injustices or conflicts that block the achievement of that harmony.

I shall end this section by saying something about the approach of the peace maker in this type of unpeaceful situation. What I shall be describing is based on the experience of myself and of people who have been carrying out the same sort of work as myself, that is Quakers and others like-minded, to whom I have referred in my book *Making Peace* as private diplomats.

Their private standing, as I have already suggested, has both advantages and disadvantages. They seldom have the equivalent of an embassy to back up their work and offer material assistance (although local well-wishers can be an excellent substitute). Nor do they have diplomatic passports and other similar advantages. On the other hand they are not bound by a 'line' they must follow, whether they believe in it or not, and the reputation they can build up for friendly impartiality is of incomparable value in tackling complex and sensitive issues of conflict, enmity and misunderstanding.

Another great asset of peace makers of this sort is that they are involved out of concern for everyone in the situation. Thus they have the strength of commitment to carry them through arduous and nerve-wracking work which could otherwise be a deadly and exhausting chore. By the same token they have feelings of warmth towards all those with whom they have dealings. When I have visited someone who might have been described as an 'awkward customer', I have tried to reject that description and to go in the spirit of meeting a friend whom I like and respect. It is remarkable what a difference this makes to human contact; it becomes alive and warm. I have also reminded myself of the strain, anguish and fear which most leaders experience in times of tension. Leaders are lonely; the more grim their circumstances, the lonelier they become. No man responsible for the conduct of hostilities can be expansive or relaxed. All his relationships are dominated by the exigencies of the struggle. Because of the sensitivity of his position, he has to be careful with whom he associates and on what terms. He may fear assassination and so withdraw even more from general contact. In any case, he is insulated by protocol from most of his people; it is a strange irony that the greater a leader's responsibility for his people the less is he in touch with those for whom he has responsibility. Thus, paradoxically, at the apex of his power he may be ill-informed, or his information may be slanted because his subordinates tell him what they think he wants to know, or because they censor the information given him about the aspect of the war with which they are concerned, or because in general they wish to present themselves in a favourable light. Leaders, in short, need friendship and support from people who they know will tell them the truth, who have no personal axe to grind, and who manifest genuine goodwill. I believe that the element of friendship between Quaker peace makers and those engaged in deadly quarrels is a crucial aspect of their role.

In this connection, I have often been asked how we handle the fact that peace making involves having a relationship, often a close relationship, with people who are committed to violent solutions to their problems. Do we tell them we disapprove of what they are doing or urge them to repent and desist? And if we don't, how do we square this with our principles? For my part I reply that I would never presume to criticise people caught up in a situation I do not share with them for the way in which they are responding to that situation. How could I, for example, preach to the oppressed of Latin America or Southern Africa? Nevertheless, I explain that I do not believe in the use of violence as either effective or moral; my job is to try to help people who can see no alternative to violence to find a substitute.

What this may mean in practice, although obviously circumstances differ, is to ask a question, although probably not as bluntly as this: why not try talking rather than shooting? The reply, not infrequently, is: we would like to but ... The task is then to analyse the nature of the 'buts' and to see if they cannot be eliminated. Some are very practical problems, such as the fear of losing the support of allies or a tactical advantage; these are usually the hardest to deal with, for the peace maker is in no position to ensure that a reduction of military momentum will not play into the hands of the other side. This 'but', however, is often hedged around with others less intractable. One type is based on unreasonable fears. These easily grow in the hot-house emotional atmosphere of conflict and sundered communications. The source of another is faulty or partial information. The Quaker peace maker is often in a position to point out why certain fears are exaggerated, that facts have been misrepresented or inadequately reported. On his/her next visit to the other side the mistake can be corrected. This is why it is often necessary for the peace maker to go round and round, hoping that on each visit a little more confusion, misapprehension or unnecessary anxiety can be dispelled.

There is another psychological element. A great deal of human behaviour is influenced by our need to have a good image of our own selves. We create for ourselves a mask representing what we would like to show to others, and to ourselves. To complement the mask is what I would call the mirage. The popular belief is that mirages are beautiful visions of palm trees and water, but anyone who has travelled in deserts knows that they live up to their dictionary definition of a false image. Mirages are shimmering stretches of livid waste. In my terms, the mirage is what we see when we squint through the slits in the mask. In order to maintain the mask, to have a gratifying self-image, we need a comparably unattractive one of our rivals or enemies. Upon them we project all the flaws and vices we fear in ourselves and try unconsciously to conceal by the mask mechanism. This gives rise to what has been termed the mirror effect, in which each protagonist sees the other in the same unfavourable light in which he himself is seen. In this way most conflicts are unreasonably exacerbated while the mutually distorted perceptions impede adequate communication, which is an essential preliminary to any accord.

Here the peace makers can play an important part. There is no need for them to spell out their feelings with what might be embarrassing frankness, but their genuine and caring concern will be felt as the kind of reassurance that obviates to some extent the need for the mask. The tension will be reduced and reasonableness and objectivity in large measure restored. Obviously peace makers must be very tactful and know enough about the situation in general to avoid using words that carry a high emotional charge. (For example, to have spoken of Biafra to members of the Federal Government of Nigeria, to whom it was a rebel territory, would have been most unwise. However, it was essential to refer to it and an acceptable synonym had to be found—a semantic problem that was in a sense trivial, but also potentially dangerous.) The reassuring goodwill of peace makers does not, of course, of itself solve any problems, but it does lay better psychological foundations for a solution. It helps to lighten the fog of negative emotions—fear, resentment, anger, jealousy, bitterness, suspicion—which renders all human conflict more intractable.

Private peace makers have to resist constant attempts to win them over to one or other of the sides. In a sense this is a measure of their acceptance; the more they are liked, the more desirable their support. The other side of this coin is that, especially if general tension rises, they may be suspected, taken to task, even upbraided, because of their relations with the other side. Peace makers can only respond, whatever the temptation and whatever their personal inclinations, with complete impartiality and unalloyed friendliness. 'How can you possibly have any truck with those monsters?' they will be asked, and regaled with horror stories of massacre and torture. They can only affirm and doggedly reaffirm that they cannot take sides with one party or the other; that they are on the side of all who are in any way suffering, that they have unconditional sympathy with all who are caught in the trap of war, whether as civilians, soldiers, or political leaders; that their only enemy is the belief that human problems can be solved through violence. In no other way can the concept of reconciliation be kept at the centre of the process of peace making.

In claiming that reconciliation should be central to peace making, I am not dismissing the other elements, the bargaining, the trade-offs, the complicated military, political and economic deals, but I don't conceive that it is the role of the Quaker peace makers to be concerned with these things in the same way as a Carrington or a Kissinger. If Quakers were to attempt comparable manoeuvres they would jeopardise their more idio-syncratic psychological and, basically, spiritual role. Their more feasible task is to work for favourable conditions in which a settlement can be sought rather than to elaborate the terms of that settlement. Clearly they cannot be indifferent to the nature of any settlement being considered, but if they espouse one solution rather than another they are in immediate danger of weakening their impartiality. If asked their opinion, they are, of course, entitled to give it. The most effective way to do this is to avoid saying that a is better than b, but to draw up a balance sheet of the implications in so far as they can see them, of the various proposals for ending the conflict. One proviso must be made. There are sometimes ways of ending the struggle by driving the conflict underground. Friends, who are naturally eager to see the end of hostilities, must be cautious of settle-ments which give a false hope of peace. I have already cited the case of Bangladesh where a settlement with West Pakistan (Bangladesh being then East Pakistan) would probably only have led to even greater violence in the future and would, in any case, have perpetuated the violence of oppression that led to the struggle.

However, although peace makers should seldom if ever be partisan advocates of particular political solutions, they should not be afraid of pointing out what, in their opinion, will not work. There may also be many issues on which their advice may be sought and their information be useful. The contestants may, for example, want—and need—to know what their opponents and neighbouring states think about specific issues. If their infor-mation on this is distorted they might make mistakes that would prolong the struggle and increase the suffering. I have on occasion found high officials surprisingly ill informed on crucial matters. Obviously peace makers have to be careful not to supply knowledge that would facilitate the waging of a campaign. Judgement must be exercised over this. More often, however, ignorance or partial knowledge only adds to the confusion and suspicion that fuel violence.

*   *   *

These last two chapters on the Practice of Peace Making have perhaps over emphasised the more 'exotic' international aspects of peace making. If so, the reason is probably because I have drawn on what seemed to me the more telling examples out of my experience, or of people known to me, such as Danilo Dolci and Paulo Freire. But I would be sad indeed if anyone were to conclude that peace making were only to be practised in this type of setting. If it were, then very few of us, including myself, would do much of it. Peace making is, however, as I have pointed out several times, a fundamental and universal human function. We are all involved, all the time, in relationships that could be more peaceful—or less so. We are constantly faced with the opportunities for peace making, for making life slightly more, or slightly less, harmonious. This applies particularly, of course, to those of us who are involved with others in the course of our work—teachers, social and community workers, nurses, doctors, trade union officials, marriage counsellors, employers, etc. I would be distressed if I thought that any such people, reading what I have written, were to say to themselves: 'That may be all very fine and interesting, but it's really nothing to do with me'. I hope that the principles I have tried to outline will be seen as having wide application. The first four I believe to be universal: we must acknowledge that of God in all with whom we have any dealings; we must listen to them and give them attention; we must earn their acceptance; we must be doggedly persistent. The second three apply to the three main types of un-peaceful relationships: in the Stage of Quiescence we must try to stimulate awareness; in the Stage of Revolution we must work, non-violently, for change; in the Conflict of Equals we must establish communication. However, although I have discussed these things separately, they represent difference of emphasis rather than separation. There is, for example, no stage when we should not work for greater awareness (particularly in ourselves), no situation in which we should not listen, or seek to be more worthy of confidence, or strive to improve understanding between those separated by conflict.

The principles I have just referred to might be thought of as the seven pillars of peace making. They support the sheltering structure of peace that gives us its protection. It is a structure we can all help to build every day of our lives. As I just said, it is quite unnecessary to be involved in some grandiose international project. It is also unnecessary, however important these roles may be, to be a social worker, nurse, etc. It is only necessary to be a human being involved with other human beings as a parent, child, neighbour, colleague. Even that is not necessary. The most impersonal contact in a shop, if we see the person serving us or whom we are serving as a real person grounded in the divine, can become an encounter that gives comfort and peace.

Peace making, as I have tried to define and describe it, consists of manifesting the truth and applying it to disordered relationships, relationships that are disordered specifically because they are not nurtured by the truth. Thus peace making is not merely the removal of what is sick or ignorant, smoothing out the crinkles of misunderstanding, but the stimulation of growth and the unfolding of all our God-given capacities.

But we should not think that peace making will bring popularity. If peace making means, and is based upon, the truth of our nature as beings made in the image and likeness of God, enshrining a particle of His nature, it will arouse hostility among many. A large proportion of humanity have been misled into believing that their happiness depends upon their possessions, position, power, prosperity and all the other adjuncts of material well-being—and even if they do not have them, they believe this and strive for them. Some, faced with a truth that proclaims something diametrically different, will abandon their illusions. Others, however, will cling to them; and the more they are threatened by reality, the more desperately they will cling. Often they will attempt to evade the threat to their precariously ill-founded sense of security by attacking the peace maker. For this reason, throughout history, many have been slain.

CONCLUSION—TRUE JUSTICE

I would like to conclude by circling back to the ideas with which I began. These could be decked out with much theological or metaphysical language, but it seems better to express them very simply: our nature is founded in God. It is this that is real, true and eternal. Everything else is transitory and illusory, for God is all. Nothing that appears contrary to God has life or meaning. Our existence only has significance in so far as it reflects and expresses God.

Our relationship with all others must be dominated by this transcendent fact. We are joined to them through the divinity of our natures and must always so act that we can together manifest it more completely.

Conditions that call for peace making, as described in Chapter 3, are ones dominated by illusion, by the false selves that are shaded from the light by a cloak of ignorance. These conditions can never be improved by adding violence or any other action that is inconsistent with the good that represents God. Indeed such activity can only compound the evil of the situation.

If anyone, including ourselves, acts unpeacefully, our first duty is to acknowledge the reality of our nature. This strikes at the roots of all unpeacefulness. We could perhaps find physical or psychological ways of preventing a person from behaving destructively, but only by evoking their true identity can the source of violence be eliminated. For those who hold the views expressed in the first two chapters, this approach is the foundation of peace making.

Peace making is a combination of right thinking and right

action that flows from this approach. In the last two chapters, I tried to describe the practical approach that follows from the philosophy. This approach was divided between general principles, and practices appropriate to specific types of unpeaceful relationships.

If we believe in that of God in every one, we must treat all as we would be treated, with love, respect and intelligent concern, no matter what they have done or are doing. We must remember that their bad actions are not themselves; that whatever they do, they are grounded in the divinity that is the sole reality. We must try to help them move from ignorance to knowledge, from hatred to love. We may have to prevent them in their ill-doing, but if we act with love, there could be no greater service; we may hope that others may so act towards us.

If we hold a different view of human nature, believing it to be intrinsically evil, steeped in original sin, violent, 'animal', imperfect, or a Manichean mixture of good and bad, our behaviour will certainly differ in dealing with unpeaceful relations. The emphasis will shift from acknowledging the divine essence in those whose actions are unpeaceful, and acting to restore them to an understanding of their true selves, to changing those actions. Depending on circumstances we would try to persuade, manipulate, or control, even to intimidate, restrain forcibly, or to kill. This would be impossible to those who recognised our shared heritage, our unity as beings made in the image and likeness of God. But to those who do not, or do so half-heartedly, the desire to alter material circumstances may legitimise such action in the name of maintaining or restoring peace.

Finally, I would like to return to the beginning of this work, and consider its title. This is drawn, of course, from the passage in the Epistle of James which reads: 'True justice is the harvest reaped by peace makers from seeds sown in the spirit of peace'.

The verses immediately following are those to which George Fox refers in his declaration to the Commonwealth Commissioners (both quoted on page 53) speaking of the spirit that takes away the occasion of wars and the rapacity that foments them. None can doubt that justice is the proper fruit of peace making, while materialistic greed, leading to gross inequities, is a prime source of violence.

I have tried to show that without justice there is no peace; even in the absence of open strife, there is no peace, only a manipulated lull in hostilities. Justice has two connotations. One is fairness, righteous dealing, integrity; necessary, but not sufficient preconditions for lasting peace. The other, to quote the *Oxford English Dictionary*, is 'observance of the divine law; righteousness; the state of being just before God'. When the bonding force of love unifies these two dimensions, the temporal and the spiritual, the task of the peace maker is fulfilled. Peace has been established: true justice reigns.

BIBLIOGRAPHY

Spiritual Writings

J. A. Arberry, *Sufism*. London: Allen & Unwin, 1950

Farid ud-din Attar, *The Conference of Birds* (Mantiq ut-Tair) trns. C. S. Nott. New York: Samuel Weisser, 1954. This twelfth-century prose poem is a magnificent expression of Sufism.

Sydney Bailey, 'The Christian Vocation of Reconciliation' in *Crucible: the Journal of the Board for Social Responsibility of the General Synod of the Church of England*, July/September, 1979

Howard H. Brinton, *Friends for 300 years*. Pendle Hill Publications, 1952, rptd. 1964

William Blake, *Poems*.

Chuang Tzu, *The Complete Works of Chuang Tzu* trns. by Burton Watson. New York: Columbia U.P., 1968

The Cloud of Unknowing (Author unknown, probably lived in the fourteenth century) trns. and introd. Clifton Walters. London: Penguin Classics, 1961

The Dhammapada (Probably compiled in the third century BC) trns. J. Mascaro. London: Penguin Classics, 1973

Meister Eckhart, *Sermons, etc*. trns. C. de B. Evans. London: Watkins, 1924

Mary Baker Eddy, *Science and Health: with key to the scriptures*. Boston: First Church of Christ, 1875

George Fox, *Journal* ed. John Nickalls. London Yearly Meeting, 1952, rptd. 1975 (This is the most readily available edition, but I have the edition edited, introduced and annotated by Rufus M. Jones published by Capricorn Books, New York, 1963)

George Fox, *Epistles*. Most readily available selection is *No more but my love: letters of George Fox* selected and edited by Cecil W Sharman. London: Quaker Home Service, 1980

The Gospel according to Thomas trns. A. Guillaumont, et. al. London: Collins, 1959

Bede Griffiths, *Return to the Centre*. London: Collins/Fount, 1976.

Jelalud-din Rumi, *Masnavi i Ma'navi: the spiritual couplets of Jelalu* trns. E. H. Whinfield. Octagon, 1898, rptd. 1974

St. John of the Cross, *The Dark Night of the Soul*, trns. and ed. E. Allison Peers. Newman Press, 1934 (I prefer this edition of all those I have seen)

William Johnston, *The Inner Eye of Love*. London: Collins/Fount, 1978

Rufus M. Jones, *An Interpretation of Quakerism*. London: Quaker Home Service, 1930, rptd. 1979

Julian of Norwich, *Revelations of Divine Love*. London: Penguin Classics, 1966. This was written after a mystical experience in 1373

C. G. Jung, *Memories, Dreams, Reflections*. London: Collins/Fontana, 1967

Martin Luther King, *A Martin Luther King Treasury*. New York: Educational Heritage, 1964

Lao Tzu, *Tao Te Ching*. London: Penguin Classics, 1963. Lao Tzu, who may have been the author, probably wrote about 500 BC.

William Law, *A Serious call to a Devout and Holy Life*. London: Dent, 1975, and *The Spirit of Prayer, Spirit of Love*. Cambridge: James Clarke, 1967

Wolf Mendl, *Prophets and Reconcilers: reflections on the Quaker Peace Testimony*. London: Quaker Home Service, 1974

Thomas Merton, *Mystics and Zen Masters*. New York: Dell Pub., 1960

P. U. Ouspensky, *In Search of the Miraculous*. New York: Harcourt, 1949

Jan van Ruysbroeck. *John of Ruysbroeck* ed. and introd. by Evelyn Underhill. Westminster, Md., USA: Christian Classics, 1974. This appears to be the only currently available English language edition of the great fourth century mystic's writings. It contains three of his most important works, 'The adornment of the spiritual marriage', 'The sparkling stone' and 'The book of supreme truth'.

Idries Shah, *The Way of the Sufi*. London: Penguin Books, 1974. This is useful for the long extracts from great Sufi writers which are not otherwise easily found.

Swami Shankara, *Crest-Jewel of Discrimination*. Trns. and Introd. by Swami Prabhavananda and Christopher Isherwood. London: Mentor Books, 1970

Douglas Steere, *On being present where you are*. Pendle Hill Pamph.

151. Wallingford, Pa., USA: Pendle Hill, 1967

Thomas Traherne, *Poems*. London: Dobell, 1903

Evelyn Underhill, *Mysticism*. London: Methuen, rpt. 1979

The Upanishads trns. from the Sanskrit with an Introduction by Juan Mascaro. Penguin Classics, 1965. Also a useful edition *The Ten Principle Upanishads* trns. by Shree Purchit Swami and W. B. Yeats. London: Faber, 1937, rpt. 1970

Way of a Pilgrim trns. R. M. French. London: SPCK, 1972

John Woolman. *Journal and Essays of John Woolman* ed. A. M. Gummere. London: Macmillan, 1922. *Journal and Major Essays of John Woolman* ed. Phillips Moulton, Oxford U.P., 1971. *The Wisdom of John Woolman* by Reginald Reynolds. London: QHS, rpt. 1972

Mike C. H. Yarrow, *Quaker Experiences in International Conciliation*. New Haven, USA: Yale U.P., 1978

Non-violent action and social change

Joan Bondurant, *Conquest of Violence: the Gandhian philosophy of conflict*. Oxford U.P., 1958

Helder Camara, *Revolution through Peace*. London: Harper & Row, 1971

Danilo Dolci, *The Man who Plays Alone* trns. Cowan. New York: Pantheon Books, 1969

Paulo Freire, *Pedagogy of the Oppressed* trns. Myra Bergman Ramos. New York: Herder, 1970

Paulo Freire, *Cultural Action for Freedom*. Cambridge, Mass. USA: Harvard Educ. Review and Centre for Studies in Educ. and Development, 1970

Johan Galtung, *Feudalism, Structural Violence and the Structural Theory of Violence*. Paper prepared for the 3rd General Conference of the International Peace Research Assn., Karlovy Vary, Czechoslovakia

Johan Galtung, *Essays in Peace Research*, I-V. Copenhagen: Eilers, 1975-80

M. K. Gandhi. *The Collected Works of Mahatma Gandhi*. Delhi, India: Publications Div. Ministry of Information, Govnt. of India, 1958. This series at present in progress will include over 50 vols.

M. K. Gandhi, *An Autobiography: or the story of my experiments with Truth*, trns. Mahadev Desai. Ahmedabad, India: Navajivan, 1959

George Lakey, *Strategy for a Living Revolution.* Oxford: W. H. Freeman, 1973

James McNeish, *Fire Under the Ashes: the life of Danilo Dolci.* London: Hodder, 1965

Gene Sharp, *The Politics of Non-Violent Action.* Boston: Porter Sargent, 1973

Human Nature

Robert Ardrey, *The Territorial Imperative: a personal enquiry into the animal origins of property and nations.* London: Collins/Fontana, 1969

Erich Fromm, *The Anatomy of Human Destructiveness.* London: Penguin Books, 1977

Konrad Lorenz, *On Aggression.* London: Methuen, 1966

Abraham Maslow, *Towards a Psychology of Being.* Princeton, NJ, USA: Van Nostrand, 1968. Maslow was one of very few psychologists of repute whose work was directed towards demonstrating that human potential, and hence the reality of human nature, was far higher than average human achievement.

Ashley Montague, *Man and Aggression.* Oxford University Press, 1968

Desmond Morris, *The Naked Ape.* London: Mayflower, 1977.

Anthony Storr, *Human Aggression.* London: Allen Lane, 1969